图书在版编目（CIP）数据

生如夏花：泰戈尔经典诗选. ②：汉英对照 / （印）泰戈尔著；朱润译. -- 北京：新世界出版社，2016.12
ISBN 978-7-5104-6050-0

Ⅰ. ①生… Ⅱ. ①泰… ②朱… Ⅲ. ①英语—汉语—对照读物②诗集—印度—现代 Ⅳ. ①H319.4：I

中国版本图书馆CIP数据核字（2016）第280143号

生如夏花：泰戈尔经典诗选②

| 作　　者：[印] 泰戈尔
| 译　　者：朱　润
| 责任编辑：丁　鼎
| 责任印制：李一鸣　高　金
| 出版发行：新世界出版社
| 社　　址：北京西城区百万庄大街24号（100037）
| 发行部：（010）6899 5968　　（010）6899 8705（传真）
| 总编室：（010）6899 5424　　（010）6832 6679（传真）
| http://www.nwp.cn
| http://www.nwp.com.cn
| 版权部：+8610 6899 6306
| 版权部电子信箱：nwpcd@sina.com
| 印　　刷：北京旭丰源印刷技术有限公司
| 经　　销：新华书店
| 开　　本：880mm×1230mm　1/32
| 字　　数：200千字　印张：8.5
| 版　　次：2016年12月第1版　2016年12月第1次印刷
| 书　　号：ISBN 978-7-5104-6050-0
| 定　　价：39.80元

版权所有，侵权必究
凡购本社图书，如有缺页、倒页、脱页等印装错误，可随时退换。
客服电话：（010）6899 8638

给读者的话

拉宾德拉纳特·泰戈尔（Rabindranath Tagore，1861—1941），印度著名作家、诗人、哲学家和社会活动家，是世界上最多产、最富才学的作家之一，被称为"亚洲第一诗人"。

泰戈尔生于印度西孟加拉邦加尔各答的一个地主家庭，父亲是一位热衷于宗教和社会改革运动的哲学家，兄弟姐妹则都是诗人、画家等艺术爱好者。在充满文学与艺术氛围的家庭环境熏陶之下，泰戈尔从13岁起便开始写诗，醉心文学创作，并在杂志上发表作品。

在长达半个多世纪的创作生涯中，泰戈尔拥有大量的作品，这些作品涉足诗歌、小说、戏剧等领域，且均获得了杰出成就。这些作品中，共有五十多部诗集、十余部中长篇小说、百余篇短篇小说、二十多部剧本，以及不计其数的文学、哲学、政治论著。泰戈尔最为世人所知的作品，是于1913年出版的英译本《吉檀迦利》，他以此成为亚洲第一个获诺贝尔文学奖的作家。

泰戈尔对中国有着特殊而又深厚的感情，他十分热爱中国和中国的文化，曾三度到访中国，并与梁启超、梅兰芳、徐志摩等人结下了深厚的友谊。泰戈尔作品在中国的流传，更是深刻影响了中国近现代文学的进程。许多著名作家在文学创作上受泰戈尔影响甚多，例如郭沫若与他的《天上的街市》，冰心与她的《繁星》与《春水》。

《生如夏花：泰戈尔经典诗选②》收录了泰戈尔的两部代表诗作：《园丁集》与《流萤集》。本书中，编者在已出版的泰戈尔作品的基础上做了进一步修改和增补，并采用中英双语方式编写，配以毕沙罗、霍默、茹科夫斯基等世界巨匠的画作，使本书更具收藏价值。

　　《园丁集》是泰戈尔重要的代表著作之一，是由泰戈尔从自己于19世纪90年代创作的《金船集》《梦幻集》《缤纷集》《刹那集》等孟加拉文诗集中，挑选英译而成，是一部被称作"生命之歌"和"青春恋歌"的抒情诗集。内容纯净清新，融合了诗人青春时代的体验，描绘了爱情中的酸甜苦辣，同时又富于哲理，向世人回答了人生的意义、人该如何生活等问题。

　　《流萤集》来源于泰戈尔的中国和日本之行。在他的旅途中，人们常常要求他亲笔把他的思想写在扇子和绢素上。这部诗集主要歌颂了"萤火虫"一类的渺小虫儿，表达了泰戈尔对微小却勇敢、倔强的生命的赞扬，同时也以这些小虫比喻诗人自己，展现了诗人自己如流萤一般，在黑暗中不畏艰险、充满希望、勇敢前行的精神。

　　冰心曾说过："泰戈尔的诗名远远超过了他的国界。"就让我们一同在这本书当中，感受泰戈尔的睿智、慈爱与伟大吧！

THE GARDENER　　　001
园丁集

FIREFLIES　　　193
流萤集

THE GARDENER
园丁集

1

仆　人　请对你的仆人开恩吧,我的女王!

女　王　集会已经开过并且我的仆人们都走了。为什么你来得这么晚呢?

仆　人　你与别人谈过后,就是我的时间了。
　　　　我来问问有什么剩余的工作,好让你的最后一个仆人去做。

女　王　这么晚了你还期望做什么呢?

仆　人　让我做你花园里的园丁吧。

女　王　这是什么蠢想法呢?

仆　人　我要舍弃别的工作。
　　　　我把剑矛扔在尘土里。请不要派遣我去遥远的宫廷;不要命令我从事新的征讨。只求你让我做花园里的园丁吧。

女　王　你的职责是什么呢?

仆　人　为你空闲的日子服务。
　　　　我将保持你早晨散步的草径清新舒爽,你每一移步将有甘于就死的繁花来欢迎你的双足以赞颂。
　　　　我将在七叶树的枝间摆动你的秋千,傍晚的月亮将挣扎着从叶隙里亲吻你的衣裙。
　　　　我将把你床边的灯盏添满香油,我将用檀香和番红花膏为你的脚凳装饰上奇妙的图样。

女　王　　你要什么作为报酬呢？

仆　人　　只要你允许我像握着柔嫩的菡萏一般握住你的小拳，把花串套在你的纤腕上；允许我用无忧花的红汁来轻染你的脚底，用亲吻来拂去那偶然间留在那里的尘埃就可以了。

女　王　　你的祈祷被接受了，我的仆人，你将是我花园里的园丁。

Servant	HAVE mercy upon your servant, my queen!
Queen	The assembly is over and my servants are all gone. Why do you come at this late hour?
Servant	When you have finished with others, that is my time.
	I come to ask what remains for your last servant to do.
Queen	What can you expect when it is too late?
Servant	Make me the gardener of your flower garden.
Queen	What folly is this?
Servant	I will give up my other work.
	I throw my swords and lances down in the dust. Do not send me to distant courts; do not bid me undertake new conquests. But make me the gardener of your flower garden.
Queen	What will your duties be?
Servant	The service of your idle days.
	I will keep fresh the grassy path where you walk in the morning, where your feet will be greeted with praise at every step by the flowers eager for death.

> I will swing you in a swing among the branches of the saptaparna, where the early evening moon will struggle to kiss your skirt through the leaves.
> I will replenish with scented oil the lamp that burns by your bedside, and decorate your footstool with sandal and saffron paste in wondrous designs.

Queen   What will you have for your reward?
Servant   To be allowed to hold your little fists like tender lotus-buds and slip flower chains over your wrists; to tinge the soles of your feet with the red juice of ask ok a petals and kiss away the speck of dust that may chance to linger there.
Queen   Your prayers are granted, my servant, your will be the gardener of my flower garden.

2

"啊,诗人,夜晚临近;你的头发已变斑白。"

"在你孤寂的沉思中听到来生的消息了吗?"

"夜晚了,"诗人说,"虽夜已晚,我还在静听,因为也许有人会在村落中呼唤。"

"我静看着,是否有年轻的飘游的心会聚在一起,两对渴望的眼睛乞求有音乐来打破沉默,并为他们说话。"

"如果我坐在生命的岸边默想死亡和来世,又有谁来为他们编织充满激情的诗歌呢?"

"早现的晚星隐匿了。"

"葬礼柴堆中的辉光在沉静的河边慢慢地熄灭。"

"残月的微光下,胡狼在荒废的房子的庭院里齐声哀嚎。"

"假如有游子离开家,到这来守夜,低头聆听黑暗的私语,有谁会把生命的秘密在他耳边轻诉呢,如果我关上门,试图远离尘世的牵扰?"

"我的头发变斑白是件小事。"

"我永远如村里最年轻的人一样年轻,如最年老的人一样年老。"

有些人眼中含笑,甜美纯净;有些人目光闪烁,狡黠善变。

"有些人在白天流眼泪,有些人在黑暗中隐藏眼泪。"

"他们都需要我,我没有时间去沉思来生。"

"我和每一个人都是同龄的,我的头发变斑白了又怎样呢?"

"AH, poet, the evening draws near; your hair is turning grey.

"Do you in your lonely musing hear the message of the hereafter?"

"It is evening," the poet said," and I am listening because some one may call from the village, late though it be.

"I watch if young straying hearts meet together, and two pairs of eager eyes beg for music to break their silence and speak for them.

"Who is there to weave their passionate songs, if I sit on the shore of life and contemplate death and the beyond?

"The early evening star disappears.

"The glow of a funeral pyre slowly dies by the silent river.

"Jackals cry in chorus from the courtyard of the deserted house in the light of the worn-out moon.

"If some wanderer, leaving home, come here to watch the night and with bowed head listen to the murmur of the darkness, who is there to whisper the secrets of life into his ears if I shutting my doors, should try to free myself from mortal bonds?

"It is a trifle that my hair is turning grey.

"I am ever as young or as old as the youngest and the oldest of this village.

"Some have smiles, sweet and simple, and some a sly twinkel in their eyes."

"Some have tears that well up in the daylight, and others tears that are hidden in the gloom.

"They all have need for me, and I have no time to brood over the after life.

"I am of an age with each, what matter if my hair turns grey?"

3

早晨我把网撒在海里。

我从黑暗的深渊里拉出奇形奇美的东西——有些像微笑般闪亮,有些像眼泪般闪光,有些像新娘的双颊般晕红。

当我带着一天的负担回到家的时候,我的爱人正坐在花园里悠闲地扯着花的叶子。

我迟疑了一会儿,就把我捞的一切放在了她的脚前,沉默地站着。

她瞥了一眼说:"这是些什么怪东西?不知道这些东西有什么用!"

我羞愧地低下头,心想:"我并没有为这些去奋斗,这些也不是从市场买来的;这不是送给她的礼物。"

整个晚上我把这些东西一件一件地丢到了街上。

早晨行路人过来,他们把这些捡起带到远方去了。

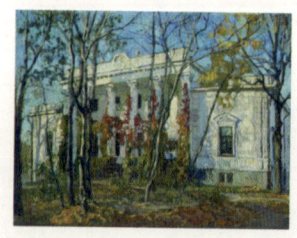

In the morning I cast my net into the sea.

I dragged up from the dark abyss things of strange aspect and strange beauty—some shone like a smile, some glistened like tears, and some were flushed like the cheeks of a bride.

When with the day's burden I went home, my love was sitting in the garden idly tearing the leaves of a flower.

I hesitated for a moment, and then placed at her feet all that I had dragged up, and stood silent.

She glanced at them and said, "What strange things are these? I know not of what use they are!"

I bowed my head in shame and thought, "I have not fought for these, I did not buy them in the market; they are not fit gifts for her."

Then the whole night through I flung them one by one into the street.

In the morning travellers came; they picked them up and carried them into far countries.

4

啊，为什么他们把我的房子建在通向市镇的路边呢？
他们把满载的船拴在我的树上。
他们任意地来回游逛。
我坐着看他们，我的光阴都浪费了。
我不能把他们打发走。于是我的日子就过去了。
日日夜夜他们的脚步声在我门前回荡。
我徒然地喊道："我不认识你们。"
有些人是我的手指认识的，有些人是我的鼻孔认识的，我脉管中的血液似乎认得他们，有些人是我的魂梦认识的。
我不能把他们打发走。我呼唤他们说："谁愿意到我房子里来就请来吧。对，来吧。"
清晨，庙里的钟声响起。
他们拿着篮子来了。
他们的脚是玫瑰红色。熹微的晨光照在他们脸上。
我不能把他们打发走。我呼唤他们说："到我的花园里采花吧。到这里来吧。"
中午，锣声在庙殿门前响起。
我不知道他们为什么放下工作在我篱畔流连。
他们发上的花已经褪色凋谢了，他们横笛里的音调也显得疲倦。
我不能把他们打发走。我呼唤他们说："我的树荫

下是清凉的。来吧,朋友们。"

夜里蟋蟀在林中鸣叫。

是谁慢慢地来到我的门前轻轻地敲?

我模糊地看到他的脸,他一句话也没说,四围的天空是静默的。

我不能打发走我沉默的客人。我在黑暗中望着他的脸,梦想的时间过去了。

Ah me, why did they build my house by the road to the market town?

They moor their laden boats near my trees.

They come and go and wander at their will.

I sit and watch them; my time wears on.

Turn them away I cannot. And thus my days pass by.

Night and day their steps sound by my door.

Vainly I cry, "I do not know you."

Some of them are known to my fingers, some to my nostrils, the blood in my veins seems to know them, and some are known to my dreams.

Turn them away I cannot. I call them and say, "Come to my house whoever chooses. Yes, come."

In the morning the bell rings in the temple.

They came with baskets in their hands.

Their feet are rosy-red. The early light of dawn is on their faces.

Turn them away I cannot. I call them and I say, "Come to my garden to gather flowers. Come hither."

In the mid-day the gong sounds at the palace gate.

I know not why they leave their work and linger near my hedge.

The flowers in their hair are pale and faded; the notes are languid in their flutes.

Turn them away I cannot. I call them and say, "The shade is cool under my trees. Come, friends."

At night the crickets chirp in the woods.

Who is it that comes slowly to my door and gently knocks?

I vaguely see the face, not a word is spoken, the stillness of the sky is all around.

Turn away my silent guest I cannot. I look at the face through the dark, and hours of dreams pass by.

5

我心神不宁。我渴望遥远的事物。

我的灵魂在渴望中走出,要去摸触模糊的远方的边缘。

哦,"伟大的来生",哦,你笛声高亢的呼唤!

我忘却了,我曾经忘却了,我没有高飞的翅膀,我永远被系在这点上了。

我渴望而又清醒,我是个异乡的异客。

你的气息向我低诉出一个不可能的希望。

我的心懂得你的语言,就像它懂得自己的语言一样。

哦,遥远的追寻,哦,你笛声热切的呼唤!

我忘却了,我曾经忘却了,我不认得路,我也没有带翼的马。

我心神不宁,我是自己心中的流浪者。

在疲惫时光的日霭中,你广大的幻象在蔚蓝的天空中呈现!

哦,最远的尽头,哦,你笛声热切的呼唤!

我忘却了,我的确忘却了,在我独居的房子里,所有的门窗都是紧闭的!

I am restless. I am athirst for faraway things.

My soul goes out in a longing to touch the skirt of the dim distance.

O Great Beyond, O the keen call of thy flute!

I forget, I ever forget, that I have no wings to fly, that I am bound in this spot evermore.

I am eager and wakeful, I am a stranger in a strange land.

Thy breath comes to me whispering an impossible hope.

Thy tongue is known to my heart as its very own.

O Far-to-seek, O the keen call of thy flute!

I forget, I ever forget, that I know not the way, that I have not the winged horse.

I am listless, I am a wanderer in my heart.

In the sunny haze of the languid hours, what vast vision of thine takes shape in the blue of the sky!

O Farthest end, O the keen call of thy flute!

I forget, I ever forget, that the gates are shut everywhere in the house where I dwell alone!

6

驯服的鸟在笼里,自由的鸟在林中。

时间到了,他们相见,这是命中注定的。

自由的鸟说:"哦,我的爱人,让我们飞到林中去吧。"

笼中的鸟低语:"到这里来吧,让我们都住在笼里。"

自由的鸟说:"在栅栏中间,哪有展翅飞翔的空间呢?"

"可怜,"笼中的鸟说,"在天空中我不知道到哪里去栖息。"

自由的鸟呼唤说:"我亲爱的,唱起森林之歌吧。"

笼中的鸟说:"坐在我旁边吧,我将教你学问人的话语。"

自由的鸟呼唤说:"不,啊,不!歌曲是永远都不可能教会的。"

笼中的鸟说:"可怜的我啊,我不会唱森林之歌。"

他们的爱情因渴望而更加浓烈,但是他们永远不能比翼双飞。

他们隔栏相望,而他们相知的愿望是没有结果的。

他们在依恋中鼓翼,唱道:"靠近些吧,我的爱人!"

自由的鸟呼唤说:"这是做不到的,我怕笼子紧闭的门。"

笼里的鸟低语:"啊,我的翅膀是无力的并且已经死去了。"

The tame bird was in a cage, the free bird was in the forest.

They met when the time came, it was a decree of fate.

The free bird cries, "O my love, let us fly to wood."

The cage bird whisper, "Come hither, let us both live in the cage."

Says the free bird, "Among bars, where is there room to spread one's wings?"

"Alas," cries the cage bird, "I should not know where to sit perched in the sky."

The free bird cries, "My darling, sing the songs of the woodlands."

The cage bird says, "Sit by my side, I'll teach you the speech of the learned."

The forest bird cries, "No, ah no! songs can never be taught."

The cage bird says, "Alas for me, I know not the songs of the woodlands."

Their love is intense with longing, but they never can fly wing to wing.

Through the bars of the cage they look, and vain is their wish to know each other.

They flutter their wings in yearning, and sing, "Come closer, my love!"

The free bird cries, "It cannot be, I fear the closed doors of the cage,"

The cage bird whispers, "Alas, my wings are powerless and dead."

7

哦，母亲，年轻的王子将从我们门前走过——今天早晨我怎顾得上干活呢？

教我怎样挽发，告诉我应该穿哪件衣裳。

你为什么吃惊地望着我呢，母亲？

我深知他不会抬眼瞥视我的窗户，我知道一瞬间他就要走出我的视线，只有那渐渐消失的笛声将从远处向我呜咽。

但是年轻的王子将从我们门前走过，这一刻我要穿上我最好的衣裳。

哦，母亲，年轻的王子已经从我们门前走过了，朝阳的金光在车辇上闪烁。

我从脸上揭开面纱，我从颈上扯下红玉的项链，扔在他行经的路上。

你为什么吃惊地看着我呢，母亲？

我深知他没有捡起我的项链；我知道它在他的轮下碾碎了，在尘土上留下了红印，并且没有人知道我的礼物是什么，是给谁的。

但是年轻的王子曾经从我们门前走过，我也曾经把我胸前的珍宝丢在他走来的路上了。

O mother, the young Prince is to pass by our door, —how can I attend to my work this morning?

Show me how to braid up my hair; tell me what garment to put on.

Why do you look at me amazed, mother?

I know well he will not glance up once at my window; I know he will pass out of my sight in the twinkling of an eye; only the vanishing strain of the flute will come sobbing to me from afar.

But the young Prince will pass by our door, and I will put on my best for the moment.

O mother, the young Prince did pass by our door, and the morning sun flashed from his chariot.

I swept aside the veil from my face, I tore the ruby chain from my neck and flung it in his path.

Why do you look at me amazed, mother?

I know well he did not pick up my chain; I know it was crushed under his wheels leaving a red stain upon the dust, and no one knows what my gift was nor to whom.

But the young Prince did pass by our door, and I flung the jewel from my breast before his path.

8

当我床前的灯熄灭时,我和晨鸟一同醒来。

我在散发上戴上新鲜的花环,坐在打开的窗前。

年轻的行人在玫瑰色的晨霭中从大路走来。

珠链在他的颈上,阳光洒在他的冠上。他停在我门前,用渴望的呼喊声问我:"她在哪呢?"

因为非常害羞,我不好意思说出;"她就是我,年轻的行人,她就是我。"

黄昏来到,华灯未上。

我心神不宁地编着头发。

在夕阳的余晖中年轻的行人驾着车辇来了。

他的马,嘴里喷着白沫,他的衣袍上蒙着灰尘。

他在我门前下车,用疲惫的声音问:"她在哪里?"

因为非常害羞,我不好意思说出:"她就是我,疲倦的行人,她就是我。"

那是个四月的夜晚。我的屋里亮着灯。

南风温柔地吹来。吵闹的鹦鹉在笼里睡着了。

我的胸衣和孔雀颈毛一样地华丽,我的披纱和嫩草一样地碧绿。

我坐在窗前的地上望着冷清的街道。

在幽黑的夜中我不停地低吟着:"她就是我,绝望的行人,她就是我。"

园丁集　THE GARDENER　·　025　·

When the lamp went out by my bed I woke up with the early birds.

I sat at my open window with a fresh wreath on my loose hair.

The young traveller came along the road in the rosy mist of the morning.

A pearl chain was on his neck, and the sun's ray fell on his crown.

He stopped before my door and asked me with an eager cry, "Where is she?"

For very shame I could not say, "She is I, young traveller, she is I."

It was dusk and the lamp was not lit.

I was listlessly braiding my hair.

The young traveller came on his chariot in the glow of the setting sun.

His horses were foaming at the mouth, and there was dust on his garment.

He alighted at my door and asked in a tired voice, "Where is she?"

For very shame I could not say, "She is I, weary traveller, she is I."

It is an April night. The lamp is burning in my room.

The breeze of the south comes gently. The noisy parrot sleeps in its cage.

My bodice is the colour of the peacock's throat, and my mantle is green as young grass.

I sit upon the floor at the window watching the deserted street.

Through the dark night I keep humming, "She is I, despairing traveller, she is I."

9

当我在夜里独赴爱的幽会的时候,鸟儿不语,风儿不吹,街道两旁的房屋静默地站立着。

是我自己的脚镯越走越响让我羞愧。

当我坐在阳台上倾听他的脚步声时,树叶不响,河水寂静得像熟睡的哨兵膝上的刀剑。

是我自己的心脏在狂跳——我不知道如何使它安静。

当我的爱人来了并且坐在我身边,当我的身躯颤抖,眼睫下垂,夜更深了,风吹灯灭,云片在繁星上曳过轻纱。

是我自己胸前的珠宝放出光明。我不知道怎样把它藏起。

When I go alone at night to my love-tryst, birds do not sing, the wind does not stir, the houses on both sides of the street stand silent.

It is my own anklets that grow loud at every step and I am ashamed.

When I sit on my balcony and listen for his footsteps, leaves do not rustle on the trees, and the water is still in the river like the sword on the knees of a sentry fallen asleep.

It is my own heart that beats wildly—I do not know how to quiet it.

When my love comes and sits by my side, when my body trembles and my eyelids droop, the night darkens, the wind blows out the lamp, and the clouds draw veils over the stars.

It is the jewel at my own breast that shines and gives light. I do not know how to hide it.

10

停下工作吧,新娘。听,客人已经来了。

听见没有,他在轻轻地摇动紧拴门的链子?

小心不要让你的脚镯发出声音,迎接他的时候脚步不要太急。

停下工作吧,新娘,客人在晚上已经来了。

不,这不是一阵阴风,新娘,不要惊恐。

这是四月夜中的满月,院里的影子是暗淡的,头上的天空是光亮的。

若是你觉得必要,用轻纱遮上脸。若是你觉得害怕,提着灯到门前去。

不,这不是一阵阴风,新娘,不要惊恐。

若是你害羞,不必和他说话,你迎接他的时候只需站在门边。

若他问你问题,如果你愿意,你就沉默地低下眼眸。

你提着灯,带他进来的时候,不要让手镯叮当响。

如果你害羞,不必和他说话。

工作还没有做完吗,新娘?听,客人已经来了。

你还没有把牛栏里的灯点起来吗?

你还没有把晚祷的供篮准备好吗?

你还没有在发缝中涂上鲜红的吉祥标志,你还没有打理过晚妆吗?

哦,新娘,你没听见,客人来了吗?

停下你手中的工作吧!

Let your work be, bride. Listen, the guest has come.

Do you hear, he is gently shaking the chain which fastens the door?

See that your anklets make no loud noise, and that your step is not over-hurried at meeting him.

Let your work be, bride, the guest has come in the evening.

No, it is not the ghostly wind, bride, do not be frightened.

It is the full moon on a night of April; shadows are pale in the courtyard; the sky overhead is bright.

Draw your veil over your face if you must, carry the lamp to the door if you fear.

No, it is not the ghostly wind, bride, do not be frightened.

Have no word with him if you are shy; stand aside by the door when you meet him.

If he asks you questions, and if you wish to, you can lower your eyes in silence.

Do not let your bracelets jingle when, lamp in hand, you lead him in.

Have no word with him if you are shy.

Have you not finished your work yet, bride? Listen, the guest has come.

Have you not lit the lamp in the cowshed?

Have you not got ready the offering basket for the evening service?

Have you not put the red lucky mark at the parting of your hair, and done your toilet for the night?

O bride, do you hear, the guest has come?

Let your work be!

11

　　就这样来吧,不要在梳妆上拖延了。
　　即使你的发辫松散,即使你的发缝没有分直,即使你胸衣的丝带没有系紧,都不要在意。
　　就这样来吧,不要在梳妆上拖延了。
　　来吧,快步走过草坪。
　　即使露水沾掉了你脚上的红粉,即使你踝上的铃串松散,即使你链上的珠儿脱落,都不要在意。
　　来吧,快步走过草坪。
　　你没看见云雾遮住天空了吗?
　　鹤群从遥远的河岸飞起,阵阵狂风吹过常青的灌木。
　　惊牛奔向村里的棚栏。
　　你没看见云雾遮住天空了吗?
　　你徒然点上晚妆的灯火——它颤抖着在风中熄灭了。
　　谁能看出你眼睑上没有涂眼影?因为你的眼睛比雨云更暗。
　　你徒然点上晚妆的灯火——它熄灭了。
　　就这样来吧,不要在梳妆上拖延了。
　　即使花环没有编好,谁在意呢;即使手镯没有扣上,让它去吧。
　　天空被阴云遮蔽了——时间已晚。
　　就这样来吧,不要在梳妆上拖延了。

Come as you are; do not loiter over your toilet.

If your braided hair has loosened, if the parting of your hair be not straight, if the ribbons of your bodice be not fastened, do not mind.

Come as you are; do not loiter over your toilet.

Come, with quick steps over the grass.

If the raddle come from your feet because of the dew, if the rings of bells upon your feet slacken, if pearls drop out of your chain, do not mind.

Come with quick steps over the grass.

Do you see the clouds wrapping the sky?

Flocks of cranes fly up from the further river-bank and fitful guests of wind rush over the heath.

The anxious cattle run to their stalls in the village.

Do you see the clouds wrapping the sky?

In vain you light your toilet lamp—it flickers and goes out in the wind.

Who can know that your eyelids have not been touched with lampblack? For your eyes are darker than rain-clouds.

In vain you light your toilet lamp—it goes out.

Come as you are; do not loiter over your toilet.

If the wreath is not woven, who cares; if the wrist-chain has not been linked, let it be.

The sky is overcast with clouds—it is late.

Come as you are; do not loiter over your toilet.

12

若是你要忙着灌满水瓶,来吧,哦,到我的湖上来吧。

湖水将回绕在你的脚边,汩汩地说出它的秘密。

风雨来临前的阴影投在沙滩上,云雾低垂在丛树的蓝线上,像你眉毛上的浓发。

我很熟悉你脚步的旋律,它们在我心中敲击。

来吧,哦,到我的湖上来吧,如果你必须灌满水瓶。

如果你想懒散闲坐,让你的水瓶漂浮在水面,来吧,哦,到我的湖上来吧。

草坡碧绿,野花数不胜数。

你的想法将从你乌黑的眼眸中飞出,像鸟儿飞出巢穴。

你的面纱将滑落到脚上。

来吧,哦,如果你必须要闲坐,到我的湖上来吧。

如果你想停止玩耍,跳进水里,来吧,哦,到我的湖上来吧。

把你的蓝色披风留在岸上;蔚蓝的水将没过你,藏住你。

水波将蹑足来吻你的颈脖,在你耳边低语。

来吧,哦,如果你想跳进水里,到我的湖上来吧。

如果你发狂了,想投入死亡,来吧,哦,到我的湖上来吧。

它是清凉的,深到无底。
它黑暗得像无梦的睡眠。
在它的深处黑夜就是白天,歌曲就是沉默。
来吧,哦,如果你想投入死亡,到我的湖上来吧。

If you would be busy and fill your pitcher, come, O come to my lake.

The water will cling round your feet and babble its secret.

The shadow of the coming rain is on the sands, and the clouds hang low upon the blue lines of the trees like the heavy hair above your eyebrows.

I know well the rhythm of your steps, they are beating in my heart.

Come, O come to my lake, if you must fill your pitcher.

If you would be idle and sit listless and let your pitcher float on the water, come, O come to my lake.

The grassy slope is green, and the wild flowers beyond number.

Your thoughts will stray out of your dark eyes like birds from their nests.

Your veil will drop to your feet.

Come, O come to my lake if you must sit idle.

If you would leave off your play and dive in the water, come, O come to my lake.

Let your blue mantle lie on the shore; the blue

water will cover you and hide you.

The waves will stand at tiptoe to kiss your neck and whisper in your ears.

Come, O come to my lake, if you would dive in the water.

If you must be mad and leap to your death, come, O come to my lake.

It is cool and fathomlessly deep.

It is dark like a sleep that is dreamless.

There in its depths nights and days are one, and songs are silence.

Come, O come to my lake, if you would plunge to your death.

13

我别无所求,只站在林边树后。
倦意还逗留在黎明的眼中,露水在空气里。
湿草的懒味悬垂在地面的薄雾中。
在榕树下,你用奶油般嫩鲜的手挤着牛奶。
我沉静地站着。
我一言不发。那是藏起的鸟儿在密叶中的歌唱。
芒果树在乡村公路上撒着繁花,蜜蜂一只一只嗡嗡地飞来。
池塘边的湿婆神庙的门是开着的,朝拜者开始吟诵。
你把罐儿放在膝上挤着牛奶。
我提着空桶站着。
我没有走向你。
天空在庙里的锣声中醒来。
街上的尘土在驱走的牛蹄下飞扬。
把汩汩发响的水罐挂在腰上,女人们从河边走来。
你的手镯叮叮当当响,泡沫溢出罐沿。
晨光渐逝而我没有走向你。

I asked nothing, only stood at the edge of the wood behind the tree.

Languor was still upon the eyes of the dawn, and the dew in the air.

The lazy smell of the damp grass hung in the thin mist above the earth.

Under the banyan tree you were milking the cow with your hands, tender and fresh as butter.

And I was standing still.

I did not say a word. It was the bird that sang unseen from the thicket.

The mango tree was shedding its flowers upon the village road, and the bees came humming one by one.

On the side of the pond the gate of Shiva's temple was open and the worshipper had begun his chants.

With the vessel on your lap you were milking the cow.

I stood with my empty can.

I did not come near you.

The sky woke with the sound of the gong at the temple.

The dust was raised in the road from the hoofs of the driven cattle.

With the gurgling pitchers at their hips, women came from the river.

Your bracelets were jingling, and foam brimming over the jar.

The morning wore on and I did not come near you.

14

我在路边行走,也不知道为什么,午时已过,竹枝在风中沙沙作响。

倾斜的影子张臂拖住流光的双足。

布谷鸟都唱倦了它们的歌曲。

我在路边行走,也不知道为什么。

低垂的树荫掩住水边的小屋。

有人正忙着工作,她的手镯在一角奏出音乐。

我站在小屋前面,不知道为什么。

狭窄的小径蜿蜒着穿过许多芥菜田和许多层芒果林。

它经过村庙和渡口的集市。

我在这茅屋面前停住了,但不知道为什么。

几年前,三月风吹的一天,当时春天倦慵地低语,芒果花掉落在灰尘中。

浪花跳起,掠过立在渡口阶沿上的铜瓶。

我想着三月风吹的这天,不知道为什么。

阴影加深,牛群归栏。

孤寂的牧场上灯光灰白,村人在岸边待渡。

我漫步回去,不知道为什么。

I was walking by the road, I do not know why, when the noonday was past and bamboo branches rustled in the wind.

The prone shadows with their out-stretched arms clung to the feet of the hurrying light.

The koels were weary of their songs.

I was walking by the road, I do not know why.

The hut by the side of the water is shaded by an overhanging tree.

Some one was busy with her work, and her bangles made music in the corner.

I stood before this hut, I know not why.

The narrow winding road crosses many a mustard field, and many a mango forest.

It passes by the temple of the village and the market at the river landing place.

I stopped by this hut, I do not know why.

Years ago it was a day of breezy March when the murmur if the spring was languorous, and mango blossoms were dropping on the dust.

The rippling water leapt and licked the brass vessel that stood on the landing step.

I think of that day of breezy March, I do not know why.

Shadows are deepening and cattle returning to their folds.

The light is grey upon the lonely meadows, and the village are waiting for the ferry at the bank.

I slowly return upon my steps, I do not know why.

15

我像麝鹿一样在林荫中奔跑,因它自己的香气发狂。

夜晚是五月正中的夜晚,清风是南国的清风。

我迷了路,徘徊着,我寻求得不到的东西,得到我没有寻求的东西。

欲望的影像从我心中走出,跳起舞来。

这影像一闪而过。

我想紧紧捉住它,它躲开我,又引着我走错。

我寻求得不到的东西,得到我没有寻求的东西。

I run as a musk-deer runs in the shadow of the forest mad with his own perfume.

The night is the night of mid-May, the breeze is the breeze of the south.

I lose my way and I wander, I seek what I cannot get, I get what I do not seek.

From my heart comes out and dances the image of my own desire.

The gleaming vision flits on.

I try to clasp it firmly, it eludes me and leads me astray.

I seek what I cannot get, I get what I do not seek.

16

　　手握着手,眼望着眼;就这样开始了我们的心路历程。

　　三月的月明之夜;空气里有凤仙花的甜蜜;我的横笛躺在地上,你的花环也没有编成。

　　你我之间的爱像歌曲一样淳朴。

　　你橘黄色的面纱使我眼睛迷醉。

　　你为我编的茉莉花环使我心激动,像受了表扬。

　　这是一个又予又留、又隐又现的游戏;有些微笑,有些羞怯,也有些甜蜜的无用的斗争。

　　你我之间的爱像歌曲一样淳朴。

　　没有当前以外的神秘,不强求做不到的事情,没有魅惑后面的阴影,没有幽暗深处的探求。

　　你我之间的爱像歌曲一样淳朴。

　　我们没有走出一切语言之外而进入永远的沉默;我们没有举起手,寻求希望以外的东西。

　　我们付出,得到,这足够了。

　　我们没有乐极生悲榨取痛苦的酒。

　　你我之间的爱像歌曲一样淳朴。

Hands cling to hands and eyes linger on eyes; thus begins the record of our hearts.

It is the moonlit night of March; the sweet smell of henna is in the air; my flute lies on the earth neglected and your garland of flowers is unfinished.

This love between you and me is simple as a song.

Your veil of the saffron colour makes my eyes drunk.

The jasmine wreath that you wove me thrills to my heart like praise.

It is a game of giving and withholding, revealing and screening again; some smiles and some little shyness, and some sweet useless struggles.

This love between you and me is simple as a song.

No mystery beyond the present; no striving for the impossible; no shadow behind the charm; no groping in the depth of the dark.

This love between you and me is simple as a song.

We do not stray out of all words into the ever silent; we do not raise our hands to the void for things beyond hope.

It is enough what we give and we get.

We have not crushed the joy to the utmost to wring from it the wine of pain.

This love between you and me is simple as a song.

17

黄鸟在树上歌唱,使我的心欢快起舞。
我们都住在一个村子里,这是我们的一份快乐。
她心爱的一对小羊,到我花园的树荫下吃草。
它们如果走进我的麦场,我就把它们抱在怀里。
我们村子名叫康遮那,人们管我们的小河叫安遮那。
我的名字村人都知道,她的名字是软遮那。
我们中间只隔着一块田野。
在我们树林里做窝的蜜蜂,飞到他们的林中去采蜜。
从他们渡头阶上流来的落花,顺水飘进了我们洗澡的池塘里。
一筐一筐的干红花从他们田地里送到我们的集市上。
我们村子名叫康遮那,人们管我们的小河叫安遮那。
我的名字村人都知道,她的名字是软遮那。
通向他们家的那条曲巷,春天弥漫着芒果花香。
当他们的亚麻籽都成熟了的时候,我们田里的苎麻正在开花。
在他们房上莞尔的星辰,送给我们同样的光亮。
在他们水槽里满溢的雨水,给我们的迦昙树林带来了喜乐。
我们村子名叫康遮那,人们管我们的小河叫安遮那。
我的名字村人都知道,她的名字是软遮那。

The yellow birds sings in their tree and makes my heart dance with gladness.

We both live in the same village, and that is our one piece of joy.

Her pair of pet lambs come to graze in the shade of our garden trees.

If they stray into my barley field, I take them up in my arms.

The name of our village is Khanjanau, and Anjana they call our river.

My name is known to all the village, and her name is Ranjana.

Only one field lies between us.

Bees that have hived in our grove go to seek honey in theirs.

Flowers launched from their landing-stairs come floating by the stream where we bathe.

Baskets of dried kusm flowers come from their fields to our market.

The name of our village is Khanjanau, and Anjanau they call our river.

My name is known to all the village, and her name is Ranjanau.

The lane that winds to their house is fragrant in the spring with mango flowers.

When their linseed is ripe for harvest the hemp is in bloom in our field.

The stars that smile on their cottage send us the same twinkling look.

The rain that floods their tank makes glad our kadam forest.

The name of our village is Khanjanau and Anjanau they call our river.

My name is known to all the village, and her name is Ranjanau.

18

　　当这两姊妹出去打水的时候,她们来到这里笑了。

　　她们一定察觉到,每次她们出来打水时,站在树后的那个人儿。

　　当姊妹俩走过这里的时候,她们互相耳语。

　　她们一定猜到了,每当她们出来打水时,站在树后的那个人的秘密。

　　当她们走到这里的时候,水瓶忽然倾倒,水流出来了。

　　她们一定发现,每逢她们出来打水时,站在树后的那个人的心正在跳着。

　　当她们来到这里的时候,姊妹俩相互瞥了一眼又笑了。

　　她们飞快的脚步中带着笑声,使这个每次她们出来打水时站在树后的人儿心脑混乱了。

When the two sisters go to fetch water, they come to this spot and they smile.

They must be aware of somebody who stands behind the trees whenever they go to fetch water.

The two sisters whisper to each other when they pass this spot.

They must have guessed the secret of that somebody who stands behind the trees whenever they go to fetch water.

Their pitchers lurch suddenly, and water spills when they reach this spot.

They must have found that somebody's heart is beating who stands behind the trees whenever they go to fetch water.

The two sisters glance at each other when they come to this spot, and they smile.

There is a laughter in their swift-stepping feet, which makes confusion in somebody's mind who stands behind the trees whenever they go to fetch water.

19

你腰间挂着灌满的水瓶,在河边路上行走。

你为什么迅速地转头,从飘扬的面纱里偷偷地看我?

这个从黑暗中向我送来的一瞥,像凉风在粼粼的微波上掠过,一阵震颤直到阴凉的岸边。

它向我飞来,像夜中的小鸟急速地穿过无灯的屋子两边打开的窗户,又在黑夜中消失了。

你像一颗藏在山后的星,我是路上的行人。

但是为什么你停了一下,从面纱中瞥见我的脸,当你腰间挂着灌满的水瓶在河边路上行走的时候?

You walked by the riverside path with the full pitcher upon your hip.

Why did you swiftly turn your face and peep at me through your fluttering veil?

That gleaming look from the dark came upon me like a breeze that sends a shiver through the sipping water and sweeps away to the shadowy shore.

It came to me like a bird of the evening that hurriedly flies across the lampless room from the one open window to the other, and disappears in the night.

You are hidden like a star behind the hills, and I am a passer-by upon the road.

But why did you stop for a moment and glance at my face through your veil while you walked by the riverside path with the full pitcher upon your hip?

20

他天天来了又走。
去吧,把我头上的花朵送去给他吧,我的朋友。
假如他问送花的人是谁,请你不要把我的名字告诉他,因为他来了又要走的。
他坐在树下的地上。
用繁花密叶给他铺一个座位吧,我的朋友。
他的眼神是忧伤的,它把忧伤带到了我的心中。
他没有说出他的心事,他只是来了又走了。

Day after day he comes and goes away.
Go, and give him a flower from my hair, my friend.
If he asks who was it that sent it, I entreat you do not tell him my name—for he only comes and goes away.
He sits on the dust under the tree.
Spread there a seat with flowers and leaves, my friend.
His eyes are sad, and they bring sadness to my heart.
He does not speak what he has in mind; he only comes and goes away.

21

年轻的游子,当天亮的时候,为什么特地来到我门前?

每次我进出经过他身旁,我的眼睛总被他的面孔吸引。

我不知道是应该和他说话还是保持沉默。他为什么特地来到我门前呢?

七月的阴夜是暗沉的;秋日的天空是浅蓝的,南风把春天吹得烦躁不安。

他每次用新调编着新歌。

我放下工作,眼里充满迷茫。他为什么特地来到我门前呢?

Why did he choose to come to my door, the wandering youth, when the day dawned?

As I come in and out I pass by him every time, and my eyes are caught by his face.

I know not if I should speak to him or keep silent. Why did he choose to come to my door.

The cloudy nights in July are dark; the sky is soft blue in the autumn; the spring days are restless with the south wind.

He weaves his songs with fresh tunes every time.

I turn from my work and my eyes fill with the mist. Why did he choose to come to my door?

22

当她快步走过我身旁时,裙的边缘触到了我。

从一颗心的无名小岛上忽然飘来了一阵春天的暖流。

一霎,搅扰的纷繁拂过我,立刻又消失了,像扯落了的花瓣在风中飘扬。

它落在我的心上,像她身体的叹息和她心灵的低语。

When she passed by me with quick steps, the end of her skirt touched me.

From the unknown island of a heart came a sudden warm breath of spring.

A flutter of a flitting touch brushed me and vanished in a moment, like a torn flower petal blown in the breeze.

It fell upon my heart like a sigh of her body and whisper of her heart.

23

为什么你悠闲地坐在那里,把手镯玩得叮当作响呢?
灌满你的水瓶,是该回家的时候了。
为什么你悠闲地搅动着水玩,偷偷地瞥视路上的行人呢?
灌满水瓶回家吧。
早晨的时光过去了——暗黑的水不断地流逝。
波浪互相低语嬉笑闲玩着。
飘荡的云朵聚集在远野高地的天边。
它们留恋着、悠闲地看着你的脸微笑着。
灌满水瓶回家吧。

Why do you sit there and jingle your bracelets in mere idle sport?

Fill your pitcher. It is time for you to come home.

Why do you stir the water with your hands and fitfully glance at the road for some one in mere idle sport?

Fill your pitcher and come home.

The morning hours pass by—the dark water flows on.

The waves are laughing and whispering to each other in mere idle sport.

The wandering clouds have gathered at the edge of the sky on yonder rise of the land.

They linger and look at your face and smile in mere idle sport.

Fill your pitcher and come home.

24

不要把你心里的秘密藏起来,我的朋友!

对我说吧,秘密地只对我一个人说吧。

你笑得这样温婉,说话这样轻柔,我的心会倾听你的话语,而不是我的耳朵。

夜深沉,庭静默,鸟巢也被睡眠笼罩着。

从犹豫的泪里,从沉吟的笑里,从甜美的羞怯和痛苦里,把你心底的秘密告诉我吧!

Do not keep to yourself the secret of your heart, my friend!

Say it to me, only to me, in secret.

You who smile so gently, softly whisper, my heart will hear it, not my ears.

The night is deep, the house is silent, the birds' nests are shrouded with sleep.

Speak to me through hesitating tears, through faltering smiles, through sweet shame and pain, the secret of your heart.

25

"到我们这来吧,年轻人,诚实地告诉我们,为什么你眼里带着疯癫?"

"我不知道我喝了什么野罂粟花酒,而使我的眼里带着疯癫。"

"啊,多难为情!"

"好吧,有人聪明有人愚笨,有人细心有人马虎。有的眼睛会笑,有的眼睛会哭——我的眼睛带着疯癫。"

"年轻人,你为什么这样凝立在树影下呢?"

"我的脚被我负重的心压得倦乏了,我就在树影下凝立着。"

"啊,多难为情!"

"好吧,有人一直前进,有人到处流连,有人是自由的,有人是被束缚的——我的脚被我负重的心压得倦乏了。"

"Come to us, youth, tell us truly why there is madness in your eyes?"

"I know not what wine of wild poppy I have drunk, that there is this madness in my eyes."

"Ah, shame!"

"Well, some are wise and some foolish, some are watchful and some careless. There are eyes that smile and eyes that weep—and madness is in my eyes."

"Youth, why do you stand so still under the shadow of the tree?"

"My feet are languid with the burden of my heart, and I stand still in the shadow."

"Ah, shame!"

"Well, some march on their way and some linger, some are free and some are fettered—and my feet are languid with the burden of my heart."

26

"从你慷慨的手中所给予的,我都接受。别无所求。"

"是的,是的,我懂你,谦卑的乞丐,你是乞求一个人的所有。"

"如果你给我一朵残花,我也要将它戴在心上。"

"要是那花上有刺呢?"

"我就忍着。"

"是的,是的,我懂你,谦卑的乞丐,你是乞求一个人的所有。"

"若是你只对我的脸投来一次怜爱的目光,就会让我的生命直到死后还是甜蜜的。"

"倘若那只是残酷的眼光呢?"

"我就让它永远刺穿我的心。"

"是的,是的,我懂你,谦卑的乞丐,你是乞求一个人的所有。"

"What comes from your willing hands I take. I beg for nothing more."

"Yes, yes, I know you, modest mendicant, you ask for all that one has."

"If there be a stray flower for me I will wear it in my heart."

"But if there be thorns?"

"I will endure them."

"Yes, yes, I know you, modest mendicant, you ask for all that one has."

"If but once you should raise your loving eyes to my face it would make my life sweet beyond death."

"But if there be only cruel glances?"

"I will keep them piercing my heart."

"Yes, yes, I know you, modest mendicant, you ask for all that one has."

27

"即使爱只给你带来了悲伤,也不要关上你的心。"

"啊,不,我的朋友,你的话语太深沉了,我不理解。"

"心是应该和一滴泪、一首歌一起送人的,我的罪人。"

"啊,不,我的朋友,你的话语太深沉了,我不理解。"

"喜悦就像露珠一样的脆弱,在欢笑中死去。悲伤却是强大而持久的。让哀愁的爱在你眼中苏醒吧。"

"啊,不,我的朋友,你的话语太深沉了,我不理解。"

"莲花盛开在阳光下,丢弃了它的所有。在永恒的冬霭里,它将不再含苞。"

"啊,不,我的朋友,你的话语太深沉了,我不理解。"

"Trust love even if it brings sorrow. Do not close up your heart."

"Ah no, my friend, your words are dark, I cannot understand them."

"The heart is only for giving away with a tear and a song, my love."

"Ah no, my friend, your words are dark, I cannot understand them."

"Pleasure is frail like a dewdrop, while it laughs it dies. But sorrow is strong and abiding. Let sorrowful love wake in your eyes."

"Ah no, my friend, your words are dark, I cannot understand them."

"The lotus blooms in the sight of the sun, and loses all that it has. It would not remain in bud in the eternal winter mist."

"Ah no, my friend, your words are dark, I cannot understand them."

28

你疑问的眼神是忧郁的。它似乎了解我的意思,就好像月亮探测大海。

我已经将生命全都暴露在你眼前,没有任何隐藏和保留。因此你不认识我。

如果它只是一块宝石,我就能把它碎成千百粒,串成项链戴在你的颈上。

倘若它只是一朵花,圆圆的、小小的、香香的,我就能从枝上采下戴在你的发上。

然而它是一颗心,我的爱人。哪里才是它的边和底?

你不知道这个王国的界限,但你仍是女王。

假使它只是片刻的欢乐,它将在喜悦中开花,你立刻就会看到、懂得。

若它只是一阵痛苦,它将融化成晶莹的泪滴,不着一字地反映出它最深处的秘密。

可是它是爱,我的爱人。

它的欢愉和苦痛是无边的,它的需求和财富是无尽的。

它和你亲近得像生命一样,但你永远不能完全理解它。

Your questioning eyes are sad. They seem to know my meaning as the moon would fathom the sea.

I have bared my life before your eyes from end to end, with nothing hidden or held back. That is why you know me not.

If it were only a gem I could break it into a hundred pieces and string them into a chain to put on your neck.

If it were only a flower, round and small and sweet, I could pluck it from its stem to set it in your hair.

But it is a heart, my beloved. Where are its shores and its bottom?

You know not the limits of this kingdom, still you are its queen.

If it were only a moment of pleasure it would flower in an easy smile, and you could see it and read it in a moment.

If it were merely a pain it would melt in limpid tears, reflecting its inmost secret without a word.

But it is love, my beloved.

Its pleasure and pain are boundless, and endless its wants and wealth.

It is as near to you as your life, but you can never wholly know it.

29

　　对我说吧,我的爱人!用语言告诉我你唱的是什么。
　　夜晚是黑暗的,星星消失在云里,风在叶丛中叹息。
　　我将散开我的头发,我青蓝的披风将像黑夜那样紧裹着我。我要把你的头紧抱在我的怀里:在甜美的寂寥中你的心在低诉。我将闭目静听。我不会盯着你的脸。
　　等你的话讲完了,我们要静默凝坐。只有丛树在黑暗中低语。
　　夜将发白。天将破晓。我们将要望望彼此的眼睛,然后各走各的路。
　　对我说吧,我的爱!用语言告诉我你唱的是什么。

Speak to me, my love! Tell me in words what you sang.

The night is dark. The stars are lost in clouds. The wind is sighing through the leaves.

I will let loose my hair. My blue cloak will cling round me like night. I will clasp your head to my bosom; and there in the sweet loneliness murmur on your heart. I will shut my eyes and listen. I will not look in your face.

When your words are ended, we will sit still and silent. Only the trees will whisper in the dark.

The night will pale. The day will dawn. We shall look at each other's eyes and go on our different paths.

Speak to me, my love! Tell me in words what you sang.

30

你是夜晚的一朵云,在我梦幻的天空浮动。

我永远用爱恋的渴想来描绘你。

你是我一个人的,我一个人的,我无尽梦想中的住客!

你的双脚被我心底热切渴望的光染得绯红,我落日之歌的搜集者!

我的痛苦之酒让你的唇儿苦甜。

你是我一个人的,我一个人的,我寂寥梦想中的住客!

我用热情的浓影染黑了你的眼,我凝视深处的访客!

我抓住了你,缠住了你,我的爱人,在我音乐的网里。

你是我一个人的,我一个人的,我永生梦想中的住客!

You are the evening cloud floating in the sky of my dreams.

I paint you and fashion you ever with my love longings.

You are my own, my own, Dweller in my endless dreams!

Your feet are rosy-red with the glow of my heart's desire, Gleaner of my sunset songs!

Your lips are bitter-sweet with the taste of my wine of pain.

You are my own, my own, Dweller in my lonesome dreams!

With the shadow of my passion have I darkened your eyes, Haunter of the depth of my gaze!

I have caught you and wrapt you, my love, in the net of my music.

You are my own, my own, Dweller in my deathless dreams!

31

我的心,这只野鸟,在你的眼中找到了它的天空。
它们是清晨的摇篮,是星辰的王国。
我的歌声在它们的深处消失。
让我在那天空翱翔吧,在那孤寂的无垠天际。
让我冲破它的云层,在它的日照中展翅吧。

My heart, the bird of the wilderness, has found its sky in your eyes.

They are the cradle of the morning, they are the kingdom of the stars.

My songs are lost in their depths.

Let me but soar in that sky, in its lonely immensity.

Let me but cleave its clouds and spread wings in its sunshine.

32

告诉我,这一切是否都是真的。我的爱人,告诉我,这是否是真的。

当这一双眼睛闪出电光,你胸中的阴云发出暴风般的回答。

我的唇儿真像觉醒的初恋的蓓蕾那样甜蜜吗?

消失了的五月回忆仍然萦绕在我的肢体上吗?

大地真的像一张竖琴,因为我双足的踏触而颤抖成歌声吗?

那么当我看见从夜的眼睛里掉下露珠时,晨光会真的因为围绕我的身躯而感到快乐吗?

是真的吗,是真的吗,你的爱穿越时代、世界来找寻我吗?

当你最后找到我时,你天长地久的渴望,在我的温柔的话语里,在我的眼睛、嘴唇和飘扬的长发里,找到了完全的安宁吗?

那么无尽的神秘真的写在我小小的额上吗?

告诉我,我的爱人,这一切是否都是真的呢。

Tell me if this be all true, my lover, tell me if this be true.

When these eyes flash their lightning the dark clouds in your breast make stormy answer.

Is it true that my lips are sweet like the opening bud of the first conscious love?

Do the memories of vanished months of May linger in my limbs?

Does the earth, like a harp, shiver into songs with the touch of my feet?

Is it then true that the dewdrops fall from the eyes of night when I am seen, and the morning light is glad when it wraps my body round?

Is it true, is it true, that your love travelled alone through ages and worlds in search of me?

That when you found me at last, your age-long desire found utter peace in my gentle speech and my eyes and lips and flowing hair?

Is it then true that the mystery of the Infinite is written on this little forehead of mine?

Tell me, my lover, if all this be true.

33

我爱你,我的爱人。请宽恕我的爱。

像一只迷路的鸟,我被俘获了。

当我的心震动时,它丢了面纱,变得赤裸。用怜悯覆盖它吧,爱人,请宽恕我的爱。

如果你不能爱我,爱人,请宽恕我的苦痛。

请不要远远地斜视我。

我会偷偷回到我的角落里去,在阴暗中坐下。

我将用双手遮掩起我赤裸的惭愧。

转过脸去吧,我的爱人,请宽恕我的苦痛。

假如你爱我,爱人,请宽恕我的快乐。

当我的心被愉快的洪水卷走时,不要笑我危险的放纵。

当我坐在宝座上,用我肆虐的爱来控制你时,当我像女神一样向你施恩时,宽恕我的傲慢吧,爱人,也宽恕我的欢愉。

I love you, beloved. Forgive me my love.

Like a bird losing its way I am caught.

When my heart was shaken it lost its veil and was naked. Cover it with pity, beloved, and forgive me my love.

If you cannot love me, beloved, forgive me my pain.

Do not look askance at me from afar.

I will steal back to my corner and sit in the dark.

With both hands I will cover my naked shame.

Turn your face from me, beloved, and forgive me my pain.

If you love me, beloved, forgive me my joy.

When my heart is borne away by the flood of happiness, do not smile at my perilous abandonment.

When I sit on my throne and rule you with my tyranny of love, when like a goddess I grant you my favor, bear with my pride, beloved, and forgive me my joy.

34

不要不辞而别,我的爱人。
我看守了一整夜,现在我的眼睛睡意浓重。
我只怕在睡梦中丢掉你。
不要不辞而别,我的爱人。
我惊坐起伸出双手去触摸你,我问自己:"这是一个梦吗?"
但愿我能用心拴住你的双足,紧抱在胸前!
不要不辞而别,我的爱人。

Do not go, my love, without asking my leave.

I have watched all night, and now my eyes are heavy with sleep.

I fear lest I lose you when I am sleeping.

Do not go, my love, without asking my leave.

I start up and stretch my hands to touch you. I ask myself, "Is it a dream?"

Could I but entangle your feet with my heart and hold them fast to my breast!

Do not go, my love, without asking my leave.

35

只怕我太容易认识你,你对我耍花招。
你用爽朗的笑声来掩藏你的泪水让我中招。
我知道,我知道你的妙招。
你从来不说出你想要说的话。
只怕我不珍惜你,你千方百计地躲避我。
只怕我把你和大家混在一起,
你独自站在一边。
我知道,我知道你的妙招。
你从来不走你要走的路。
你的要求比任何人都多,因此你才沉默。
你用俏皮的无心来避开我的赠予。
我知道,我知道你的妙招。
你从来不肯接受你想要的东西。

Lest I should know you too easily, you play with me.

You blind me with flashes of laughter to hide your tears.

I know, I know your art.

You never say the word you would.

Lest I should not prize you, you elude me in a thousand ways.

Lest I should confuse you with the crowd, you stand aside.

I know, I know your art.

You never walk the path you would.

Your claim is more than that of others, that is why you are silent.

With playful carelessness you avoid my gifts.

I know, I know your art.

You never will take what you would.

36

　　他低语:"我的爱人,抬起眼睛吧。"
　　我严厉地责骂他说:"走!"但是他不动。
　　他站在我面前拉住我的手。我说:"离开我!"但是他没有走。
　　他把脸靠近我耳边。我瞪了他一眼说:"真不知羞耻!"但是他没有动。
　　他的嘴唇碰到我的脸颊。我颤抖着说:"你太大胆了!"但是他并不觉得羞耻。
　　他把一朵花戴在我发上。我说:"这也没用!"但是他站着不动。
　　他拿下我颈上的花环就走开了。我哭泣着问我的心:"他为什么不回来了?"

He whispered, "My love, raise your eyes."

I sharply chid him, and said "Go!"; but he did not stir.

He stood before me and held both my hands. I said, "Leave me!"; but he did not go.

He brought his face near my ear. I glanced at him and said, "What a shame!"; but he did not move.

His lips touched my cheek. I trembled and said, "You dare too much"; but he had no shame.

He put a flower in my hair. I said, "It is useless!"; but he stood unmoved.

He took the garland from my neck and went away. I weep and ask my heart, "Why does he not come?"

37

"你愿意把你的鲜花花环挂在我的颈上吗,佳人?"

"但是你要明白,我编的花环是为大家的,为那些偶然瞥见的人,或者那些住在未开发的大地上的人,或者住在诗人歌曲里的人。"

现在来请求我的心作为赠答已经太晚了。

曾经,我的生命像一朵蓓蕾,它所有的芬芳都贮藏在花的心里。

现在它已散发到远方。

谁知道什么魅力才可以把它们收集封闭起来呢?

我的心不许我只给一个人,它是要给很多人的。

Would you put your wreath of fresh flowers on my neck, fair one?

But you must know that the one wreath that I had woven is for the many, for those who are seen in glimpses, or dwell in lands unexplored, or live in poets' songs.

It is too late to ask my heart in return for yours.

There was a time when my life was like a bud, all its perfume was stored in its core.

Now it is squandered far and wide.

Who knows the enchantment that can gather and shut it up again?

My heart is not mine to give to one only, it is given to the many.

38

我的爱人,从前有一天,你的诗人把一首伟大史诗装进他的心里了。

唉,是我不小心,它击在你叮当响的脚镯上而引起悲楚。

它裂成诗歌的碎片散落在你的脚边。

我满载古代战争的货物,被笑浪颠簸,被泪水浸透而下沉。

你必须补偿我的损失,我的爱人。

如果我死后不朽的光荣的希望都破灭了,那就在生前让我不朽吧。

我不会为这损失伤心,也不会责备你。

My love, once upon a time your poet launched a great epic in his mind.

Alas, I was not careful, and it struck your ringing anklets and came to grief.

It broke up into scraps of songs and lay scattered at your feet.

All my cargo of the stories of old wars was tossed by the laughing waves and soaked in tears and sank.

You must make this loss good to me, my love.

If my claims to immortal fame after death are shattered, make me immortal while I live.

And I will not mourn for my loss nor blame you.

39

整个早晨我尝试编一个花环,但是花儿滑落了。

你坐在一旁偷偷地从眼角窥探我。

问这一双暗黑的恶作剧的眼睛,这是谁的错。

我尝试唱一支歌,但唱不出来。

一个暗笑在你唇上颤动,问它我失败的原因。

让你微笑的唇儿发个誓,说我的歌声如何消失在沉默里,像荷花里沉醉的蜜蜂。

夜晚了,是花瓣合起来的时候了。

允许我坐在你的旁边吧,允许我的唇儿在沉默中、在星辰的微光中做能做的工作吧。

I try to weave a wreath all the morning, but the flowers slip and they drop out.

You sit there watching me in secret through the corner of your prying eyes.

Ask those eyes, darkly planning mischief, whose fault it was.

I try to sing a song, but in vain.

A hidden smile trembles on your lips, ask of it the reason of my failure.

Let your smiling lips say on oath how my voice lost itself in silence like a drunken bee in the lotus.

It is evening, and the time for the flowers to chose their petals.

Give me how to sit by your side, and bid my lips to do the work that can be done in silence and in dim light of stars.

40

当我来向你告别的时候,一个怀疑的微笑在你眼中闪烁。

我这样做的次数太多了,以至于你认为我很快又会回来的。

说实话,我自己心里也有相同的疑问。

由于春天年年到来,满月离别后又来到,花儿每年都会在枝上红晕着脸,很可能我来向你告别只为了要再回到你身边。

然而让这幻想停留一会儿吧,不要粗暴匆忙地撵走它。

当我说要永远离开你的时候,就当作事实来接受吧,让泪雾暂时加深你眼边的黑影吧。

当我再回来的时候,随便你怎样嘲笑吧。

An unbelieving smile flits on your eyes when I come to you to take my leave.

I have done it so often that you think I will soon return.

To tell you the truth I have the same doubt in my mind.

For the spring days come again time after time; the full moon takes leave and comes on another visit, the flower come again and blush upon their branches year after year, and it is likely that I take my leave only to come to you again.

But keep the illusion awhile; do not send it away with ungentle haste.

When I say I leave you for all time, accept it as true, and let a mist of tears for one moment deepen the dark rim of your eyes.

Then smile as archly as you like when I come again.

41

我想对你说出我要说的最深的话语,但是我不敢,我怕你的哂笑。
因此我嘲笑自己,把我的秘密在玩笑中粉碎。
我把痛苦说得轻松,因为怕你会这样做。
我渴望对你说出我要说的真心的话语,但是我不敢,我怕你不相信。
因此我弄真成假,说出与我真心话相反的话。
我把痛苦说得可笑,因为我怕你会这样做。
我想用最珍贵的词汇来形容你,但是我不敢,我怕得不到同等的珍视。
因此我给了你苛刻的名字,来夸示我的硬骨。
我伤害你,因为怕你永远不理解我的痛苦。
我渴望沉静地坐在你身旁,但是我不敢,怕我的心会跳上我的唇。
因此我轻松地说东讲西,把我的心藏在言语里。
我粗暴地应付我的痛苦,因为我怕你会这样做。
我渴望从你身边走开,但是我不敢,怕你看出我的怯懦。
因此我昂起头,漫不经心地走到你面前。
从你眼里频频投来的刺激,使我的痛苦永久新鲜。

园丁集　THE GARDENER　·　097　·

I long to speak the deepest words I have to say to you; but I dare not, for fear you should laugh.

That is why I laugh at myself and shatter my secret in jest.

I make light of my pain, afraid you should do so.

I long to tell you the truest words I have to say to you; but I dare not, being afraid that you would not believe them.

That is why I disguise them in untruth, saying the contrary of what I mean.

I make my pain appear absurd, afraid that you should do so.

I long to use the most precious words I have for you; but I dare not, fearing I should not be paid with like value.

That is why I give you hard names and boast of my callous strength.

I hurt you, for fear you would never know any pain.

I long to sit silent by you; but I dare not lest my heart come out at my lips.

That is why I prattle and chatter lightly and hide

my heart behind words.

I rudely handle my pain, for fear you should do so.

I long to go away from your side; but I dare not, for fear my cowardice should become known to you.

That is why I hold my head high and carelessly come into your presence.

Constant thrusts from your eyes keep my pain fresh for ever.

42

哦，疯狂的、头号的醉汉；
如果你踢开门户在大众面前装疯；
如果你一夜间清空包袋，对慎重轻蔑地弹着指头；
如果你走在奇怪的道路上，和无用的东西游戏；
不理会韵律和逻辑；
如果你在风暴前扬起船帆，把船舵折成两半。
那么我就跟随你，伙伴，喝得烂醉走向堕落。
我在稳重明智的邻居间虚度了日日夜夜。
过多的知识让我的头发白了，过多的观察使我视力模糊了。
多年来我积攒了许多零碎的东西：
把这些东西砸碎，在上面跳舞，把它们散落到风中去吧。
因为我知道喝得烂醉而走向堕落是最大的智慧。
让一切歪曲的顾虑灭亡吧，让我无望地迷失路途吧。
让一阵旋风吹来，把我连同船锚一起卷走吧。
世界上住着贤德的人，劳动的人，有用又精明的人。
有的人从容地走在前头，有的人庄重地走在后面。
让他们愉悦繁荣吧，让我笨拙无用吧。
因为我知道喝得烂醉而走向堕落，是一切工作的结局。
此刻我誓将一切要求，让给正人君子。

我抛弃学识的自豪和是非对错的判断力。
我打碎记忆的瓶壶,挥洒最后的泪水。
用红果酒的泡沫来洗澡,照亮我的笑声。
我暂且撕裂温恭和稳重的标志。
我发誓将做一个没有价值的人,喝得烂醉而走向堕落灭亡。

O mad, superbly drunk;

If you kick open your doors and play the fool in public;

If you empty your bag in a night, and snap your fingers at prudence;

If you walk in curious paths and play with useless things;

Reck not rhyme or reason;

If unfurling your sails before the storm you snap the rudder in two.

Then I will follow you, comrade, and be drunken and go to the dogs.

I have wasted my days and nights in the company of steady wise neighbors.

Much knowing has turned my hair grey, and much watching has made my sight dim.

For years I have gathered and heaped up scraps and fragments of things:

Crush them and dance upon them, and scatter them all to the winds.

For I know this the height of wisdom to be drunken and go to the dogs.

Let all crooked scruples vanish, let me hopelessly

lose my way.

Let a gust of wild giddiness come and sweep me away from my anchors.

The world is peopled with worthies, and workers, useful and clever.

There are men who are easily first, and men who come decently after.

Let them be happy and prosper, and let me be foolishly futile.

For I know this the end of all works to be drunken and go to the dogs.

I swear to surrender this moment all claims to the ranks of the decent.

I let go my pride of learning and judgment of right and of wrong.

I'll shatter memory's vessel, scattering the last the drop of tears.

With the foam of the berry-red wine I will bathe and brighten my laughter.

The badge of the civil and staid I'll tear into shreds for the nonce.

I'll take the holy vow to be worthless, to be drunken and go to the dogs.

43

不,我的朋友,我永远不会做个苦行者,随便你怎么说。

假如她不和我一起受戒,我永远不会做一个苦行者。

这是我坚定的决心,如果我找不到一个阴凉的住所和一个忏悔的伴侣,我永远也不会变成一个苦行者。

不,我的朋友,我永远不会离开我的炉火与家庭,去退隐到深林里曲;如果仕林阴中没有欢笑的呼应;如果没有郁金色的衣裙在风中飘扬;如果它的幽静不因为轻语而加深。

我永远也不会做一个苦行者。

No, my friends, I shall never be an ascetic, whatever you may say.

I shall never be an ascetic if she does not take the vow with me.

It is my firm resolve that if I cannot find a shady shelter and a companion for my penance, I shall never turn ascetic.

No, my friends, I shall never leave my hearth and home, and retire into the forest solitude, if rings no merry laughter in its echoing shade and if the end of no saffron mantle flutters in the wind; if its silence is not deepened by soft whispers.

I shall never be an ascetic.

44

　　尊敬的长者，宽恕这一对罪人吧。

　　今天春风猖狂地跳起旋舞，把尘土和枯叶都卷走了，你的功课也随着一起失去了。

　　前辈，不要说生命是空虚的。

　　我已经和死亡订下一次约定，仅仅在这一段芬芳的时光中，我们已变为不朽。

　　即使是国土的军队凶暴地前来追捕，我们也会忧伤地摇摇头说："兄弟们，你们打扰我们了。"如果你们一定要做这个嘈杂的游戏，到别处去敲击你们的武器吧。

　　因为我们刚在这稍纵即逝的时光中变成永恒。

　　如果友善的人们来把我们围起来，我们应该恭敬地向他们鞠躬说，这个荣幸使我们惭愧。在我们居住的无尽天空之下，没有多少空间。因为春天繁花盛放，蜜蜂忙碌的翅翼也彼此摩肩接踵。只住着我们两个仙人的小天堂，狭窄得太可笑了。

Reverend sir, forgive this pair of sinners.

Spring winds today are blowing in wild eddies, driving dust and dead leaves away, and with them your lessons are all lost.

Do not say, father, that life is a vanity.

For me have made truce with death for once, and only for a few fragrant hours, we two have been made immortal.

Even if the king's army came and fiercely fell upon us, we should sadly shake our heads and say, "Brothers, you are disturbing us." If you must have this noisy game, go and clatter your arms elsewhere.

Since only for a few fleeting moments we have been made immortal.

If friendly people came and flocked around us, we should humbly bow to them and say, "This extravagant good fortune is an embarrassment to us." Room is scare in the infinite sky where we dwell. For in the springtime flowers come in crowds, and the busy wings of bees jostle each other. Our little heaven, where dwell only we two immortals, is too absurdly narrow.

45

对那些一定要离开的客人们,请求神帮他们快走,并且除掉他们所有的足迹。

把舒服的、单纯的、亲近的微笑一起拥进你的怀里。

今天是幻象的节日,他们不知道自己的死期。

让你的笑声只作为无意义的欢笑,像闪光的涟漪。

让你的生命像露珠在叶尖一样,在时光的边缘轻舞。

在你的琴弦上弹出阵阵即兴的节奏吧。

To the guests that must go bid God's speed and brush away all traces of their steps.

Take to your bosom with a smile what is easy and simple and near.

To-day is the festival of phantoms that know not when they die.

Let your laughter be but a meaningless mirth like twinkles of light on the ripples.

Let your life lightly dance on the edges of Time like dew on the tip of a leaf.

Strike in chords from your harp fitful momentary rhythms.

46

你离开我,自己上路了。

我想我会为你哀伤,还将用金色的诗歌锻成你孤寂的形象,供养在我心里。

但是呀,我的运气很坏,时间很仓促。

青春一年一年地消逝;春日是短暂的;柔弱的花朵毫无意义地凋谢,精明的人警告我说,生命只是莲叶上的一颗露珠。

我应该忽视这些,只凝视着背弃我的那个人吗?

这会是无礼的、蠢笨的,因为时光太短暂了。

那么,来吧,我雨夜滴答的脚步声;微笑吧,我金色的秋天;来吧,无虑无忧的四月,到处分发你的亲吻吧。

你来吧,还有你,也有你!

我的爱人们,你知道我们都是凡人。为一个带走她心的人而心碎,是件精明的事吗?因为时光是短暂的。

坐在角落沉思,将你们是我的世界都写在旋律里,是甜美的。

把哀伤紧抱,决不受人宽慰,是英勇的。

但是一个新鲜的面庞,在我门外窥视,抬起眼来看我的眼。

我只能拭掉眼泪,更改我歌曲的调子。

因为时光是短暂的。

You left me and went on your way.

I thought I should mourn for you and set your solitary image in my heart wrought in a golden song.

But ah, my evil fortune, time is short.

Youth wanes year after year; the spring days are fugitive; the frail flowers die for nothing, and the wise man warns me that life is but a dewdrop on the lotus leaf.

Should I neglect all this to gaze after one who has turned her back on me?

That should be rude and foolish, for time is short.

Then, come, my rainy nights with pattering feet; smile, my golden autumn; come, careless April, scattering your kisses abroad.

You come, and you, and you also!

My love, you know we are mortals. Is it wise to break one's heart for the one who takes her heart away? For time is short.

It is sweet to sit in a corner to muse and write in rhymes that you are all my world.

It is heroic to hug one's sorrow and determine not to be consoled.

But a fresh face peeps across my door and raises its eyes to my eyes.

I cannot but wipe away my tears and change the tune of my song.

For time is short.

47

如果你要这样,我就结束歌唱。

如果它使你的心颤抖,我就把目光从你脸上移开。

如果它让你在行走时忽然惊跳,我就躲开到别的路走。

如果它在你编织花环时使你烦乱,我就躲开你孤独的花园。

如果它让水花飞溅,我就不在你的岸边划船。

If you would have it so, I will end my singing.

If it sets your heart aflutter, I will take away my eyes from your face.

If it suddenly startles you in your walk, I will step aside and take another path.

If it confuses you in your flower-weaving, I will shun your lonely garden.

If it makes the water wanton and wild, I will not row my boat by your bank.

48

把我从你甜蜜的枷锁中放出来吧,我的爱人,不要再斟上亲吻的酒。

香烟的浓雾窒塞了我的心。

把门打开,让晨光进屋吧!

我消失在你心里,缠裹在你爱抚的折痕中。

把我从你的魔咒中释放吧,把男子气概还给我,好让我把自由的心献给你。

Free me from the bonds of your sweetness, my love! No more of this wine of kisses.

This mist of heavy incense stifles my heart.

Open the doors, make room for the morning light.

I am lost in you, wrapped in the folds of your caresses

Free me from your spells, and give me back the manhood to offer you my free heart.

49

我握住她的手,把她抱紧在怀里。

我尝试用她的可爱来填满我的怀抱,用亲吻来掠夺她的甜笑,用双眼来吸饮她深黑的一瞥。

啊,但是,它在哪儿呢?谁能从天空滤出蔚蓝呢?

我尝试去抓住美;它避开我,只有躯体留在我的手中。

困惑而疲倦地,我回来了。

躯体怎么能触到那只有精神才能触到的花朵呢?

I hold her hands and press her to my breast.

I try to fill my arms with her loveliness, to plunder her sweet smile with kisses, to drink her dark glances with my eyes.

Ah, but, where is it? Who can strain the blue from the sky?

I try to grasp the beauty, it eludes me, leaving only the body in my hands.

Baffled and weary I come back.

How can the body touch the flower which only the spirit may touch?

50

爱人,我的心日夜盼望和你相见——那像吞噬一切死亡一样的会面。

像一阵风暴把我卷走,把我的一切都带走,劈开我的睡眠掠走我的梦。剥夺了我的世界。

在这毁灭里,在精神全部的裸露里,让我们在美中合一吧。

唉,我徒劳的渴望!除了在你里面,哪有这合一的希望呢,我的神?

Love, my heart longs day and night for the meeting with you——for the meeting that is like all-devouring death.

Sweep me away like a storm; take everything I have; break open my sleep and plunder my dreams. Rob me of my world.

In that devastation, in the utter nakedness of spirit, let us become one in beauty.

Alas for my vain desire! Where is this hope for union except in thee, my God?

51

唱完最后一支歌就让我们离开吧。
当这夜过完就把它忘掉吧。
我想把谁紧抱在臂弯呢?梦是永远不会被俘虏的。
我渴望的双手把空虚紧压在心上,擦伤了我的胸膛。

Then finish the last song and let us leave.

Forget this night when the night is no more.

Whom do I try to clasp in my arms? Dreams can never be made captive.

My eager hands press emptiness to my heart and it bruises my breast.

52

灯为什么熄灭了呢?
我用斗篷遮住它,防止被风吹灭,因此灯熄了。
花为什么凋谢了呢?
我焦急的爱把它紧压在我心上,因此花谢了。
溪水为什么干涸了呢?
我盖起一道坝把它拦起来给自己用,因此溪水干了。
琴弦为什么断了呢?
我试图强弹一个它力不能胜的调子,因此琴弦断了。

Why did the lamp go out?

I shaded it with my cloak to save it from the wind, that is why the lamp went out.

Why did the flower fade?

I pressed it to my heart with anxious love, that is why the flower faded.

Why did the stream dry up?

I put a dam across it to have it for my use, that is why the stream dried up.

Why did the harp-string break?

I tried to force a note that was beyond its power, that is why the harp-string is broken.

53

你为什么盯着我使我羞怯呢?

我不是来乞讨的。

只为了要消磨时光,我才来站在你院边的花园篱笆外。

你为什么盯着我使我羞怯呢?

我没有从你的花园采下一朵玫瑰,没有摘走一颗果子。

我谦卑地在任何生客都可以站的路边树荫下,找个荫蔽。

我没有摘下一朵玫瑰。

是的,我的脚疲乏了,雨骤然而下。

风在摇曳的竹林中喊叫。

云片像败退似的跑过天空。

我的脚疲乏了。

我不知道你如何看待我,或是你在门口等什么人。

闪电昏眩了你看我的目光。

我怎会知道你能看到站在幽暗中的我呢?

我不知道你如何看待我。

白日结束,雨势停了片刻。

我离开你花园边的树荫和草地上的座位。

日光已暗,关上你的门吧,我走我的路。

白日结束了。

Why do you put me to shame with a look?

I have not come as a beggar.

Only for a passing hour I stood at the end of your courtyard outside the garden hedge.

Why do you put me to shame with a look?

Not a rose did I gather from your garden, not a fruit did I pluck.

I humbly took my shelter under the wayside shade where every strange traveller may stand.

Not a rose did I pluck.

Yes, my feet were tired, and the shower of rain came down.

The winds cried out among the swaying bamboo branches.

The clouds ran across the sky as though in the flight from defeat.

My feet were tired.

I know not what you thought of me or for whom you were waiting at your door.

Flashes of lighting dazzled your watching eyes.

How could I know that you could see me where I stood in the dark?

I know not what you thought of me.

The day is ended, and the rain has ceased for a moment.

I leave the shadow of the tree at the end of your garden and this seat on the grass.

It has darkened; shut your door; I go my way.

The day is ended.

54

市集已过,这么晚了你急急地提着篮子要到哪里去呢?

他们都挑着担子回家了,月亮从村头树隙中偷窥。

呼唤渡轮的回声从漆黑的水上传到远处野鸭安眠的沼泽。

市集已过,你提着篮子急匆匆地要到哪里去呢?

睡眠把她的手指放在大地的眼睛上。

鸦巢已静,竹叶的低语也已沉默。

劳作的人们从田间归来,把席子铺展在院子里。

市集已过,你提着篮子急匆匆地要到哪里去呢?

Where do you hurry with your basket this late evening when the marketing is over?

They all have come home with their burdens; the moon peeps from above the village trees.

The echoes of the voices calling for the ferry run across the dark water to the distant swamp where wild ducks sleep.

Where do you hurry with your basket when the marketing is over?

Sleep has laid her finger upon the eyes of the earth.

The nests of the crows have become silent, and the murmurs of the bamboo leaves are silent.

The laborers home from their fields spread their mats in the courtyards.

Where do you hurry with your basket when the marketing is over?

55

正午的时候你走了。

烈日正当空。

你走的时候,我已完成了工作,孤单地坐在凉台上。

风阵阵吹来,带来许多远野的香气。

鸽子在树荫下不知疲倦地叫唤,一只蜜蜂误入我屋里,带来许多远野的消息。

村庄在正午的热气中入睡了。路上冷冷清清。

树叶的沙沙声时起时息。

当村庄在正午的热气中入睡时,我凝望天空,把一个我知道的人的名字编织在蔚蓝里。

我忘记了把头发编起。困倦的微风在我颈上和它玩耍。

河水在树荫下平静地淌着。

懒散的白云一动不动。

我忘了编起我的头发。

正午的时候你走了。

路上灰尘炙热,田野都在喘息。

鸽子在浓荫中叫唤。

当你走的时候,我独坐在凉台上。

It was mid-day when you went away.

The sun was strong in the sky.

I had done my work and sat alone on my balcony when you went away.

Fitful gusts came winnowing through the smells of many distant fields.

The doves cooed tireless in the shade, and a bee strayed in my room humming the news of many distant fields.

The village slept in the noonday heat. The road lay deserted.

In sudden fits the rustling of the leaves rose and died.

I gazed at the sky and wove in the blue the letters of a name I had known, while the village slept in the noonday heat.

I had forgotten to braid my hair. The languid breeze played with it upon my neck.

The river ran unruffled under the shady bank.

The lazy white clouds did not move.

I had forgotten to braid my hair.

It was mid-day when you went away.

The dust of the road was hot and the fields panting.

The doves cooed among the dense leaves.

I was alone in my balcony when you went away.

56

我是众多妇女中为烦琐的日常家务而忙碌的一个。

你为什么独把我选出来,并且把我从日常生活的凉荫中带出来?

没有表达出来的爱是神圣的。它像黑暗中的宝石般在隐藏的心里闪光。在异样的日光中,它看起来昏暗得可怜。

啊,你打碎了我内心的盖子,把我战栗的爱情拖到空旷的地方,把那曾经藏我心巢的阴暗的一角毁坏了。

别的女人和从前一样。

没有一个人窥探到内心最深处,她们不知道自己的秘密。

她们轻快地微笑,哭泣,谈话,工作。她们每天到庙里去,点上灯,到河中打水。

我希望能从无遮拦的颤羞中救出我的爱情,但是你转身离去。

是的,你的前途是远大的,但是你把我的归路切断了,让我在无遮盖的眼睛日夜瞪视下的世界赤裸着。

I was one among many women busy with the obscure daily tasks of the household.

Why did you single me out and bring me away from the cool shelter of our common life?

Love unexpressed is sacred. It shines like gems in the gloom of the hidden heart. In the light of the curious day it looks pitifully dark.

Ah, you broke through the cover of my heart and dragged my trembling love into the open place, destroying for ever the shady corner where it hid its nest.

The other women are the same as ever.

No one has peeped into their inmost being, and they themselves know not their own secret.

Lightly they smile, and weep, chatter, and work. Daily they go to the temple, light their lamps, and fetch water from the river.

I hope my love would be saved from the shivering shame of the shelterless, but you turn your face away.

Yes, your path lies open before you, but you have cut off my return, and left me stripped naked before the world with its lidless eyes staring night and day.

57

我采了你的花,哦,世界!

我把它按在胸前,花上的刺扎伤了我。

白昼离去,夜色渐浓,我发现花儿凋谢了,苦痛却存留着。

更多有香有色的花将来到你这里,哦,世界!

但是我采花的时间结束了,漆黑的夜里,我没了玫瑰,只有苦痛存留着。

I plucked your flower, O world!

I pressed it to my heart and the thorn pricked.

When the day waned and it darkened, I found that the flower had faded, but the pain remained.

More flowers will come to you with perfume and pride, O world!

But my time for flower-gathering is over, and through the dark night I have not my rose, only the pain remains.

58

一天清晨,花园中一个盲女献给我一串掩在莲叶下的花环。

我把它戴在颈上,泪水涌上我的眼睛。

我吻了她,说:"你竟然如同花朵一样地盲目。

"你自己不知道你的礼物是多么美丽。"

One morning in the flower garden a blind girl came to offer me a flower chain in the cover of a lotus leaf.

I put it round my neck, and tears came to my eyes.

I kissed her and said, "You are blind even as the flowers are.

"You yourself know not how beautiful is your gift."

59

哦，女人，你不仅是神的手工艺品，而且是人的；他们常常从心里用美来打扮你。

诗人用闪光的意象为你织网，画家给你的身形以常新的不朽。

大海献上珍珠，金矿献上金子，夏日的花园献上花朵来装扮你，覆盖你，使你更加珍贵。

人类心中的愿望，已经在你的青春上洒上光荣……

你一半是女人，一半是幻梦。

O woman, you are not merely the handiwork of God, but also of men; these are ever endowing you with beauty from their hearts.

Poets are weaving for you a web with threads of golden imagery; painters are giving your form ever new immortality.

The sea gives its pearls, the mines their gold, the summer gardens their flowers to deck you, to cover you, to make you more precious.

The desire of men's hearts has shed its glory over your youth.

You are one half woman and one half dream.

60

在生命的奔腾怒吼中,哦,石头雕琢的美,你沉静无言,孤单而且冷漠。

时间迷恋地坐在你脚边低语道:

"说话吧,对我说话吧,我的爱人,说话吧,我的新娘!"

但是你的话被石头封住了,哦,不变的美!

Amidst the rush and roar of life, O Beauty, carved in stone, you stand mute and still, alone and aloof.

Great Time sits enamoured at your feet and murmurs:

"Speak, speak to me, my love; speak, my bride!"

But your speech is shut up in stone, O Immovable Beauty!

61

安静吧,我的心,让离别的时间更甜蜜吧。
让它不再是死亡,而是完满。
让爱恋融入记忆,苦痛融入诗歌吧。
让穿越天空的飞翔在巢中敛翼结束吧。
让你双手的最后碰触,像夜晚的花朵一样温柔吧。
静止别动,哦,美妙的结局,用沉默说出最后的话语吧。
我向你鞠躬,举起我的灯来照亮你的归途。

Peace, my heart, let the time for the parting be sweet.

Let it not be a death but completeness.

Let love melt into memory and pain into songs.

Let the flight through the sky end in the folding of the wings over the nest.

Let the last touch of your hands be gentle like the flower of the night.

Stand still, O Beautiful End, for a moment, and say your last words in silence.

I bow you and hold up my lamp to light you on your way.

62

在梦中朦胧的小路上,我去寻找前生的爱。

她的房子矗立在冷清的街尾。

晚风中,她宠爱的孔雀在架上昏睡着,鸽子在角落里静默着。

她把灯放在门口,站在我面前。

她抬起一双大眼睛望着我的脸,默默地问道:"你好吗,我的朋友?"

我试图回答,但是我们的语言丢失且忘记了。

我想来想去,怎么也想不起来我们的名字。

泪水在她眼中闪光,她向我伸出右手。我握住她的手沉默地站着。

我们的灯在晚风中闪烁着熄灭了。

In the dusky path of a dream I went to seek the love who was mine in a former life.

Her house stood at the end of a desolate street.

In the evening breeze her pet peacock sat drowsing on its perch, and the pigeons were silent in their corner.

She set her lamp down by the portal and stood before me.

She raised her large eyes to my face and mutely asked, "Are you well, my friend?"

I tried to answer, but our language had been lost and forgotten.

I thought and thought; our names would not come to my mind.

Tears shone in her eyes. She held up her right hand to me. I took it and stood silent.

Our lamp had flickered in the evening breeze and died.

63

行人,你一定要走吗?

夜是寂静的,黑暗在树林中昏睡。

我们的凉台上灯火通明,繁花鲜丽,青春的眼还清醒着。

你离开的时间到了吗?

行人,你一定要走吗?

我们不曾用恳求的手臂来缚住你的双足。

你的门开着。你的马也已装上了马鞍站在门外。

如果我们试图拦住你的去路,也只是用我们的歌曲。

如果我们曾想挽留你,也只用我们的眼神。

行人,我们没有希望留住你,我们只有泪滴。

在你眼里闪光的是什么样的不灭之火?

在你血管中奔流的是什么样的不息的热力?

在黑暗中有什么召唤在驱使你?

你从天上的星辰中,念到什么可怕的咒语,就是黑夜静寂而奇怪地走进你心中时带来的那个封闭的秘密的消息?

如果你不喜欢那欢乐的集会,如果你需要宁静,疲倦的心,我们就熄灭灯火,使琴无声。

我们将在黑暗里在沙沙的树叶声中静坐,乏倦的月亮将在你窗上洒下苍茫的光辉。

哦,行人,是什么不眠的精灵在午夜和你的心接触了呢?

Traveller, must you go?

The night is still and the darkness swoons upon the forest.

The lamps are bright in our balcony, the flowers all fresh, and the youthful eyes still awake.

Is the time for your parting come?

Traveller, must you go?

We have not bound your feet with our entreating arms.

Your doors are open. Your horse stands saddled at the gate.

If we have tried to bar your passage it was but with our songs.

Did we ever try to hold you back it was but with our eyes.

Traveller, we are helpless to keep you. We have only our tears.

What quenchless fire glows in your eyes?

What restless fever runs in your blood?

What call from the dark urges you?

What awful incantation have you read

among the stars in the sky, that with a sealed secret message the night entered your heart, silent and strange?

If you do not care for merry meetings, if you must have peace, weary heart, we shall put our lamps out and silence our harps.

We shall sit still in the dark in the rustle of leaves, and the tired moon will shed pale rays on your window.

O traveller, what sleepless spirit has touched you from the heart of the midnight?

64

  我在炙热的尘土的大路上消磨了一天。

  现在,在凉爽的夜晚,我敲着一个客栈的门。这客栈已经荒废坍塌了。

  一棵忧愁的菩提树,从张开裂缝的墙里伸展出饥饿的爪根。

  从前曾有过路人到这里来洗乏倦的脚。

  他们在初升月亮的微光下在院里摊开席了,坐着谈论异地的风光。

  早晨他们恢复了精神,鸟声使他们愉悦,友爱的花儿在路旁向他们点头。

  但是当我来时没有灯在等我。

  只有许多残留的灯烟熏的黑色污迹,像盲人的眼睛,从墙上瞪视着我。

  萤火虫从干涸的池边的灌木中掠过,竹枝的影子在荒芜的小径上摇曳着。

  我在一天之末做了没有主人的客人。

  我面前是漫漫的长夜,我疲乏了。

I spent my day on the scorching hot dust of the road.

Now, in the cool of the evening, I knock at the door of the inn. It is deserted and in ruins.

A grim ashath tree spreads its hungry clutching roots through the gaping fissures of the walks.

Days have been when wayfarers came here to wash their weary feet.

They spread their mats in the courtyard in the dim light of the early moon, and sat and talked of strange lands.

They woke refreshed in the morning when birds made them glad, and friendly flowers nodded their heads at them from the wayside.

But no lighted lamp awaited me when I came here.

The black smudges of smoke left by many a forgotten evening lamp stare, like blind eyes, from the wall.

Fireflies flit in the bush near the dried-up pond, and bamboo branches fling their shadows on the grass-grown path.

I am the guest of no one at the end of my day.

The long night is before me, and I am tired.

65

又是你在呼唤我吗?

夜晚来了,疲乏就像求爱的双臂围抱住我。

你叫我了吗?

我已把整天的时间给了你,残忍的主妇,你还要剥夺我的夜晚吗?

凡事都有个终结,黑暗的孤独是个人独有的。

你的声音一定要穿透黑暗来打击我吗?

难道夜晚你门前没有睡眠曲吗?

难道那披着沉默羽翼的星辰从来都不登上你无情之塔的上空吗?

难道你园中的花朵永不会在轻软的死亡中堕入尘土吗?

你一定要叫我吗,你这个不安静的人?

那就让爱的愁眼徒然地盼望和哭泣吧。

让灯盏在寂寞的屋里点亮吧。

让渡船载那些倦乏的工人回家吧。

我已经留下梦想,来赶赴你的召唤了。

Is that your call again?

The evening has come. Weariness clings round me like the arms of entreating love.

Do you call me?

I had given all my day to you, cruel mistress, must you also rob me of my night?

Somewhere there is an end to everything, and the loneness of the dark is one's own.

Must your voice cut through it and smite me?

Has the evening no music of sleep at your gate?

Do the silent-winged stars never climb the sky above your pitiless tower?

Do the flowers never drop on the dust in soft death in your garden?

Must you call me, you unquiet one?

Then let the sad eyes of love vainly watch and weep.

Let the lamp burn in the lonely house.

Let the ferry-boat take the weary labourers to their home.

I leave behind my dreams and I hasten to your call.

66

　　一个流浪的疯子在寻找点金石,他乱蓬蓬的黄褐色头发上沾满灰尘,身体瘦得像一道影子。双唇紧闭,就像他紧闭的心门,他灼烧的眼睛就像在寻找爱侣的萤火虫的光亮。

　　无边的海在他面前咆哮。

　　喧哗的波浪不停地诉说那些隐藏的宝藏,讥讽不懂得它们意义的无知。

　　也许他现在不再抱有希望了,然而他不肯休息,因为寻求已经变成他的生命——

　　就像海洋永远向天空伸着臂索求遥不可及的东西;

　　就像星辰轮回往复,却要寻求一个永远达不到的目标。

　　即便如此,那头发蓬乱沾满灰尘的疯子,依旧在那孤独的海岸漫游着寻找点金石。

　　有一天,一个村童走上来问:"告诉我,你腰上那条金链是从哪里来的呢?"

　　疯子吓了一跳——那条原来的铁链真的变成金的了;这不是一场梦,但是他不知道什么时候变成的。

　　他狂乱地敲着自己的前额——在哪里,哦,在哪里不知不觉中成功了呢?

　　捡起鹅卵石去碰碰那条链子,然后不看看变化与否,又扔掉它,这已成了习惯;就这样,疯子找到了又失去了那块点金石。

　　太阳向西方沉去,天空一片金灿灿。

　　疯子沿着自己的脚印向回走,去找寻他失去的珍宝。他气力尽消,弯曲着身体,他的心萎沉在灰尘里了,就像连根拔起的树一样。

A wandering madman was seeking the touchstone, with matted locks, tawny and dust-laden, and body worn to a shadow, his lips tight-pressed, like the shut-up doors of his heart, his burning eyes like the lamp of a glow-worm seeking its mate.

Before him the endless ocean roared.

The garrulous waves ceaselessly talked of hidden treasures, mocking the ignorance that knew not their meaning.

Maybe he now had no hope remaining, yet he would not rest, for the search had become his life,—

Just as the ocean for ever lifts its arms to the sky for the unattainable—

Just as the stars go in circles, yet seeking a goal that can never be reached—

Even so on the lonely shore the madman with dusty tawny locks still roamed in search of the touchstone.

One day a village boy came up and asked, "Tell me, where did you come at this golden chain about your waist?"

The madman started—the chain that once was iron was verily gold; it was not a dream, but he did not know when it had changed.

He struck his forehead wildly—where, O where had he without knowing it achieved success?

It had grown into a habit, to pick up pebbles and touch the chain, and to throw them away without looking to see if a change had come; thus the madman found and lost the touchstone.

The sun was sinking low in the west, the sky was of gold.

The madman returned on his footsteps to seek anew the lost treasure, with his strength gone, his body bent, and his heart in the dust, like a tree uprooted.

67

虽然夜晚缓步降临,示意一切歌声止歇;
虽然你的伙伴都去休息而你也乏倦了;
虽然恐怖在黑暗中弥漫,天空的脸也被遮上面纱;
然而,鸟儿,哦,我的鸟儿,听我的话,不要垂翅吧。

这不是林中树叶的阴影,这是大海的涨溢,像一条暗黑的蛇。
这不是盛开的茉莉花在跳舞,这是闪烁的水沫。
啊,哪里是阳光明媚的绿岸,哪里是你的窝巢?
鸟儿,哦,我的鸟儿,听我的话,不要垂翅吧。
孤单的长夜躺在你的路上,黎明在晦暗的山后昏眠。
星辰屏住呼吸地数着时光,微弱的月儿在深夜漂泛。
鸟儿,哦,我的鸟儿,听我的话,不要垂翅吧。
于你,这里没有希望,没有恐惧。
这里没有言辞,没有窃语,没有呼喊。
这里没有家,没有休息的床。
这里只有你自己的一双翅翼和无尽的天空。
鸟儿,哦,我的鸟儿,听我的话,不要垂翅吧。

Though the evening comes with slow steps and has signalled for all songs to cease;

Though your companions have gone to their rest and you are tired;

Though fear broods in the dark and the face of the sky is veiled;

Yet, bird, O my bird, listen to me, do not close your wings.

That is not the gloom of the leaves of the forest, that is the sea swelling like a dark black snake.

That is not the dance of the flowering jasmine, that is flashing foam.

Ah, where is the sunny green shore, where is your nest?

Bird, O my bird, listen to me, do not close your wings.

The lone night lies along your path, the dawn sleeps behind the shadowy hills.

The stars hold their breath counting the hours, the feeble moon swims the deep night.

Bird, O my bird, listen to me, do not close your wings.

There is no hope, no fear for you.
There is no word, no whisper, no cry.
There is no home, no bed of rest.
There is only your own pair of wings and the pathless sky.
Bird, O my bird, listen to me, do not close your wings.

68

没有人能永远活着,兄弟,也没有东西可以长久。把这谨记在心,欢欣鼓舞吧。

我们的生命不是那陈旧的重负,我们的道路不是那漫长的旅途。

一个独身的诗人,不必去唱一支古老的歌。

花儿凋零枯萎,但是戴花的人不必永远哀伤。

兄弟,把这个铭记于心,欢欣鼓舞吧。

必须有一个完全的休止符才能把完美编进音乐。

生命向它的黄昏垂落,为了沉浸于金影之中。

必须把爱从游戏中召回,饮尽悲伤的酒,再去降生于泪水的天堂。

兄弟,把这铭记于心,欢欣鼓舞吧。

我们匆忙地去采花,怕被过路的风儿偷掠。

闪夺那稍纵即逝的吻,使我们血液沸腾,双目发光。

我们的生命充满了乐趣,我们的渴望是强烈的,因为时间在奏着离别之钟。

兄弟,把这铭记于心,欢欣鼓舞吧。

我们没有时间去抓紧一件事物,压碎它又把它丢在尘土中。

时光急速地走过,把梦幻都藏于裙底。

我们的生命是短暂的,只给恋爱几天的工夫。

若是为工作和劳役,生命就变得无尽漫长。

兄弟,把这铭记于心,欢欣鼓舞吧。

美对我们是甜蜜的,因为她与我们的生命随着同样易逝的调子跳舞。

知识对我们是宝贵的,因为我们永远没有时间获取全部知识。

一切都在永恒的天堂做完。

然而大地的幻想之花,却被死亡保持得永远清新鲜丽。

兄弟,把这铭记于心,欢欣鼓舞吧。

None lives for ever, brother, and nothing lasts for long. Keep that in mind and rejoice.

Our life is not the one old burden, our path is not the one long journey.

One sole poet has not to sing one aged song.

The flower fades and dies; but he who wears the flower has not to mourn for it for ever.

Brother, keep that in mind and rejoice.

There must come a full pause to weave perfection into music.

Life droops toward its sunset to be drowned in the golden shadows.

Love must be called from its play to drink sorrow and be borne to the heaven of tears.

Brother, keep that in mind and rejoice.

We hasten to gather our flowers lest they are plundered by the passing winds.

It quickens our blood and brightens our eyes to snatch kisses that would vanish if we delayed.

Our life is eager, our desires are keen, for time tolls the bell of parting.

Brother, keep that in mind and rejoice.

There is not time for us to clasp a thing and crush it and fling it away to the dust.

The hours trip rapidly away, hiding their dreams in their skirts.

Our life is short; it yields but a few days for love.

Were it for work and drudgery it would be endlessly long.

Brother, keep that in mind and rejoice.

Beauty is sweet to us, because she dances to the same fleeting tune with our lives.

Knowledge is precious to us, because we shall never have time to complete it.

All is done and finished in the eternal Heaven.

But earth's flowers of illusion are kept eternally fresh by death.

Brother, keep that in mind and rejoice.

69

我要追捕那只金鹿。

你也许会哂笑,我的朋友,但是我追寻那躲避我的幻想。

我翻山越谷,游遍无名的土地,因为我在追捕那只金鹿。

你来市场采买,满载货物回家,但不知何时何地一阵无名之风吹到了我身上。

我心中了无牵挂,我把所有一切都抛在身后。

我翻山越谷,游遍无名的土地——我在追捕那只金鹿。

I hunt for the golden stag.

You may smile, my friends, but I pursue the vision that eludes me.

I run across hills and dales, I wander through nameless lands, because I am hunting for the golden stag.

You come and buy in the market and go back to your homes laden with goods, but the spell of the homeless winds has touched me I know not when and where.

I have no care in my heart; all my belongings I have left far behind me.

I run across hills and dales, I wander through nameless lands—because I am hunting for the golden stag.

70

我记得在童年的一天,我在水沟里漂一只纸船。
那是七月一个潮湿的日子,我独自快乐地游戏。
我在沟里漂一只纸船。
忽然间乌云密布,狂风怒号,大雨倾注而下。
小河中浑水翻腾,打沉了我的船。
我心里怨恨地想:这风暴是故意来破坏我的欢乐的,它的一切恶意都是冲着我的。
今天,七月的阴天是漫长的,我在静忆我生命中失败了的一切游戏。
当我忽然忆起我沉在沟里的纸船时,我抱怨命运,因为它多次嘲弄我。

I remember a day in my childhood I floated a paper boat in the ditch.

It was a wet of July; I was alone and happy over my play.

I floated my paper boat in the ditch.

Suddenly the storm clouds thickened, winds came in gusts, and rain poured in torrents.

Rills of muddy water rushed and swelled the stream and sunk my boat.

Bitterly I thought in my mind that the storm came on purpose to spoil my happiness; all its malice was against me.

The cloudy July day is long today, and I have been musing over all those games in life wherein I was loser.

I was blaming my fate for the many tricks it played on me, when suddenly I remembered the paper boat that sank in the ditch.

71

白日尚未结束,集市也未散去,那河岸上的集市。

我只怕我的时间被挥霍了,我最后的一文钱也丢掉了。

但是,没有,我的兄弟,我还剩余一些东西。命运并没有把我的一切都骗走。

买卖结束了。

两边的税费都收过了,是时候回家了。

但是,看门人,你要你的辛苦费吗?

别怕,我还剩余一些东西。命运并没有把我的一切都骗走。

风声预示着风暴的威胁,西方低垂的云影预报着噩兆。

寂静的河水等候着狂风。

在黑夜赶上我之前,匆忙过河。

哦,船夫,你要收费!

是的,兄弟,我还剩余一些东西。命运并没有把我的一切都骗走。

路边的树下坐着一个乞丐。可怜啊,他带着羞怯的希望望向我的脸!

他以为我带着一天的利润很富足。

是的,兄弟,我还剩余一些东西。命运并

没有把我的一切都骗走。

夜色渐深，路上寂静。萤火虫在树叶间闪烁。

谁在悄悄地蹑步跟着我？

啊，我知道，你想掠夺我的一切收获。我定不让你失望！

因为我还剩余一些东西。命运并没有把我的一切都骗走。

半夜到家。两手空空。

你带着焦虑的眼睛，在门前等我，没有睡意而沉默。

像一只羞怯的鸟，你满怀热切的爱飞进我怀抱。

唉，唉，我的神，我还剩余许多。命运并没有把我的一切都骗走。

The day is not yet alone, the fair is not over, the fair on the river-bank.

I had feared that my time had been squandered and my last penny lost.

But no, my brother, I have still something left. My fate has not cheated me of everything.

The selling and buying are over.

All the dues on both sides have been gathered in, and it is time for me to go home.

But, gatekeeper, do you ask for your toll?

Do not fear, I have still something left. My fate has not cheated me of everything.

The lull in the wind threatens storm, and the lowering clouds in the west bode no good.

The hushed water waits for the wind.

I hurry to cross the river before the night overtakes me.

O ferryman, you want your fee!

Yes, brother, I have still something left. My fate has not cheated me of everything.

In the wayside under the tree sits the beggar. Alas, he looks at my face with a timid hope!

He thinks I am rich with the day's profit.

Yes, brother, I have still something left. My fate has not cheated me for everything.

The night grows dark and the road lonely. Fireflies gleam among the leaves.

Who are you that follow me with stealthy silent steps?

Ah, I know, it is your desire to rob me of all my gains. I will not disappoint you!

For I still have something left, and my fate has not cheated me of everything.

At midnight I reach home. My hands are empty.

You are waiting with anxious eyes at my door, sleepless and silent.

Like a timorous bird you fly to my breast with eager love.

Ay, ay, my God, much remains still. My fate has not cheated me of everything.

72

几天的辛苦劳作,我盖起了一座庙宇。它没有门窗,墙壁是用厚厚的石头层层垒起的。

我忘掉其他的一切,我躲避整个世界,我凝神注视着被我安放在龛里的圣像。

里面永远是黑夜,被燃着芳香油的灯盏照亮。

袅袅的清香烟雾,把我的心缠绕在它厚重的螺旋里。

我没有睡意,用扭曲复杂的线条在墙上刻画出一些奇异的形象——带翼的马,人面的花,四肢像蛇的女子。

我没在任何地方留下一条通道,能使鸟的歌声、叶的细语或村镇的喧嚣可以进入。

在暗黑的拱顶上,唯一的声音是我祷告的回响。

我的思想变得敏锐而镇定,像尖锐的火焰。我的感官在狂喜中昏晕。

我不知时光怎样流逝,直到巨雷击中了这座庙宇,一阵剧痛刺穿我的心。

灯火显得苍白而羞愧;墙上的刻画像是被锁住的梦想,无意义地瞪视着,仿佛要躲藏起来。

我看着龛上的圣像,我看见它笑了,和神活生生地接触后活了起来。

被我囚禁的黑夜,展翅飞逝了。

With days of hard travail I raised a temple. It had no doors or windows, its walls were thickly built with massive stones.

I forgot all else, I shunned all the world, I gazed in rapt contemplation at the image I had set upon the altar.

It was always night inside, and lit by the lamps of perfumed oil.

The ceaseless smoke of incense wound my heart in its heavy coils.

Sleepless, I carved on the walls fantastic figures in mazy bewildering lines—winged horses, flowers with human faces, woman with limbs like serpents.

No passage was left anywhere through which could enter the song of birds, the murmur of leaves or hum of the busy village.

The only sound that echoed in its dark dome was that of incantations which I chanted.

My mind became keen and still like a pointed flame, my senses swooned in ecstasy.

I knew not how time passed till the thunderstone had struck the temple, and a pain stung me through the heart.

The lamp looked pale and ashamed; the carvings on the walls, like chained dreams, stared meaningless in the light as they would fain hide themselves.

I looked at the image on the altar. I saw it smiling and alive with the living touch of God.

The night I had imprisoned had spread its wings and vanished.

73

无尽的财富不属于你,我坚忍而微黑的大地母亲。
你辛劳着来填满你孩子们的嘴,但是粮食稀缺。
你给我们的欢乐礼物,从来就不是完美的。
你给孩子们做的玩具,是易碎的。
你不能满足我们所有的热切的希望,但是我能为此就背弃你吗?
你那含着苦痛阴影的微笑,在我眼中那样甜美。
你那永不枯竭的爱,对我的心如此亲切。
你是以生命的乳汁来哺育我们,而并非以那长生仙丹,因此你的眼睛永远是清醒的。
积年累月,你用色彩和诗歌来工作,但你的天堂还没有建起,仅有一丝哀伤的意味。
你创造的美上蒙着泪雾。
我将把我的诗歌倾注于你无言的内心,把我的爱倾注于你的爱中。
我将用劳动来朝拜你。
我看见过你慈爱的脸庞,我爱你的哀伤的尘土,大地之母。

Infinite wealth is not yours, my patient and dusky mother dust!

You toil to fill the mouths of your children, but food is scarce.

The gift of gladness that you have for us is never perfect.

The toys that you make for your children are fragile.

You cannot satisfy all our hungry hopes, but should I desert you for that?

Your smile which is shadowed with pain is sweet to my eyes.

Your love which knows not fulfilment is dear to my heart.

From your breast you have fed us with life but not immortality, that is why your eyes are ever wakeful.

For ages you are working with colour and song, yet your heaven is not built, but only its sad suggestion.

Over your creations of beauty there is the mist of tears.

I will pour my songs into your mute heart, and my love into your love.

I will worship you with labour.

I have seen your tender face and I love your mournful dust, Mother Earth.

74

  在世界的谒见堂里,一片淳朴的草叶,与阳光、午夜的星辰同坐在一条毯子上。
  于是,我的歌,也这样地和云彩、森林的音乐一起,在世界的心中分享席次。
  但是,你这富人,在太阳欢愉的金光中,在月亮沉思的微光中,这些纯粹的光彩中,你的财富却占不了一份。
  囊括万物的天空的祝福,并没有洒在它身上。
  当死亡降临的时候,它便会苍白凋谢,溃成尘土了。

In the world's audience hall, the simple blade of grass sits on the same carpet with the sunbeam and the stars of the midnight.

Thus my songs share their seats in the heart of the world with the music of the clouds and forests.

But, you man of riches, your wealth has no part in the simple grandeur of the sun's glad gold and the mellow gleam of the musing moon.

The blessing of the all-embracing sky is not shed upon it.

And when death appears, it pales and withers and crumbles into dust.

75

半夜,那个想成为苦行者的人宣称:

"舍家求神的时候到了。啊,谁让我留在妄想里这么久呢?"

神低语道:"我。"但是这个人的耳朵是被阻塞的。

他妻子怀里抱着熟睡的婴儿,安然地睡在床的一边。

那个人说:"是谁欺瞒了我这么久?"

那声音又道:"他们是神。"然而他也听不见。

婴儿在睡梦中啼哭,靠近他的母亲。

神命令道:"停下,傻瓜,不要离开你的家。"然而他还是听不见。

神叹息,抱怨道:"为什么我的仆人把我丢弃,又到处去寻找我呢?"

At midnight the would-be ascetic announced:

"This is the time to give up my home and seek for God. Ah, who has held me so long in delusion here?"

God whispered, "I," but the ears of the man were stopped.

With a baby asleep at her breast lay his wife, peacefully sleeping on one side of the bed.

The man said, "Who are you that have fooled me so long?"

The voice said again, "They are God," but he heard it not.

The baby cried out in its dream, nesting close to its mother.

God commanded, "Stop, fool, leave not thy home," but still he heard not.

God sighed and complained, "Why does my servant wander to seek me, forsaking me?"

76

庙前的集会正在进行。

从一大早起就开始下雨了,白天就要过去了。

比一群人的快乐还光亮的,是一个花一文钱买到一个棕榈叶哨子的小女孩的灿烂的欢笑。

响亮欢乐的哨子声,在所有的笑声与喧嚣之上飘荡。

无尽的人流拥挤在一起,道路泥泞,河水泛滥,田地都浸没在连绵不绝的雨水里。

比一群人的烦忧更深的,是一个小男孩的忧愁——他连买一根带颜色的小棍的一文钱都没有。

他凄然的眼睛盯着那间小店,使所有人的集会变得如此可怜。

The fair was on before the temple.

It had rained from the early morning and the day came to its end.

Brighter than all the gladness of the crowd was the bright smile of a girl who bought for a farthing a whistle of palm leaf.

The shrill joy of that whistle floated above all laughter and noise.

An endless throng of people came and jostled together. The road was muddy, the river in flood, the field under water in ceaseless rain.

Greater than all the troubles of the crowd was a little boy's trouble—he had not a farthing to buy a painted stick.

His wistful eyes gazing at the shop made this whole meeting of men so pitiful.

77

西边村里来的工人和他的妻子正忙着给砖窑挖土。

他们的小女儿去了河边的渡口,她无休无止地擦洗锅盘。

她的小弟弟,剃着光头,赤裸着黝黑的沾满烂泥的身躯,跟在她身后,听话地在高高的河岸上耐心地等她。

她头顶着满瓶的水,左手提着闪亮的铜壶,右手拉着那个孩子走回家去——

她是妈妈的小仆人,负重的家务使她变得庄重了。

有一天我看见那个赤裸的男孩伸着腿坐着。

他姐姐坐在水里,用一把土在转来转去地擦洗着一把水壶。

附近有一只毛茸茸的小羊,站在河岸上注视。

它走近男孩子坐着的地方,突然大叫了一声,孩子被吓得哭喊起来。

他姐姐放下手中清洗的水壶跑上岸来。

她一只手抱起弟弟,另一只手抱起小羊,把她的怜爱分成两半,人的孩子和动物的后代在深爱中联结合一了。

The workman and his wife from the west country are busy digging to make bricks of the kiln.

Their little daughter goes to the landing-place by the river; there she has no end of scouring and scrubbing of the pots and pans.

Her littler brother, with shaven head and brown, naked mud-covered limbs, follows after her and waits patiently on the high bank at her bidding.

She goes back home with the full pitcher poised on her head, the shining brass pot in her left hand, holding the child with her right—she the tiny servant of her mother, grave with the weight of the household cares.

One day I saw this naked boy sitting with legs outstretched.

In the water his sister sat rubbing a drinking-pot with a handful of earth, turning it round and round.

Near by a soft-haired lamb stood gazing along the bank.

It came close to where the boy sat and suddenly bleated aloud, and the child started up and screamed.

His sister left off cleaning her pot and ran up.

She took up her brother in one arm and the lamb in the other, and dividing her caresses between them bound in one bond of affection the offspring of beast and man.

78

这是在五月里。酷热的正午似乎无尽漫长。干渴的大地在炙热中张开了嘴。

我听到河边有个声音喊道:"来吧,亲爱的!"

我合上书打开窗向外望。

我看见一只皮毛上沾满泥土的大水牛,目光平和而耐心地站在河边;一个年轻人,站在没膝的水里,唤它去洗澡。

我高兴地笑了,一阵甜蜜在心里泛起涟漪。

It was in May. The sultry noon seemed endlessly long. The dry earth gaped with thirst in the heat.

When I heard from the riverside a voice calling, "Come, my darling!"

I shut my book and opened the window to look out.

I saw a big buffalo with mud-stained hide, standing near the river with placid, patient eyes; and a youth, knee deep in water, calling it to its bath.

I smiled amused and felt a touch of sweetness in my heart.

79

我常常在想,人和动物之间没有语言,他们心中彼此认识的界线隐藏在哪里。

在远古创世纪的早晨,经过怎样的原始乐园的简单小径,他们的心曾彼此探望过。

虽然他们的亲缘关系早已被忘记,他们恒定的足印的记号却并没有被抹去。

然而在一些无言的音乐中,忽然挪朦胧的记忆苏醒过来,野兽用温存的信任凝视着人们的脸,人们也用逗乐的心情俯视着它的眼。

就好像两个朋友戴着面具相逢,在伪装下彼此依稀地相识。

I often wonder where lie hidden the boundaries of recognition between man and the beast whose heart knows no spoken language.

Through what primal paradise in a remote morning of creation ran the simple path by which their hearts visited each other.

Those marks of their constant tread have not been effaced though their kinship has been long forgotten.

Yet suddenly in some wordless music the dim memory wakes up and the beast gazes into the man's face with a tender trust, and the man looks down into its eyes with amused affection.

It seems that the two friends meet masked and vaguely know each other through the disguise.

80

你眼睛一瞥,便能从诗人的琴弦上劫去所有诗歌的财富,端庄的女人!

但是你不屑听他们的赞美,因此我来赞颂你。

你能让世界上最骄傲的头在你脚下变得谦恭。

但是你所崇拜、所偏爱的是没有声望的人,因此我崇拜你。

你完美的双臂的碰触,能让帝王的华丽更加荣耀。

但你却用它们去除尘土,使你简陋的家整洁,因此我心中充满了敬畏。

With a glance of your eyes you could plunder all the wealth of songs struck from poets' harps, fair woman!

But for their praises you have no ear, therefore I come to praise you.

You could humble at your feet the proudest heads in the world.

But it is your loved ones, unknown to fame, whom you choose to worship, therefore I worship you.

The perfection of your arms would add glory to kingly splendour with their touch.

But you use them to sweep away the dust, and to make clean your humble home, therefore I am filled with awe.

81

你为什么这样轻声地对我耳语,哦,死神,我的死神?

当花儿夜晚凋零,牛儿回到棚房,你悄悄地来到我身边,说着我不了解的语言。

难道你一定要用昏沉的低语和凄冷的吻来追求我,来赢得我心吗,哦,死神,我的死神?

难道我们的婚礼没有隆重的仪式吗?

难道你不会在你黄褐色的卷发上系上花环吗?

难道你前面没有举旗的人吗?你没有赤红的火炬,让黑夜像火一样明亮吗,哦,死神,我的死神?

你吹着贝壳来吧,在无眠之夜来吧。

给我穿上艳红的衣服,紧握我的手带我走吧。

在我的门口备好你的车辇,让你的马焦躁嘶吼吧。

揭开我的面纱骄傲地看我的脸吧。哦,死神,我的死神!

Why do you whisper so faintly in my ears, O Death, my Death?

When the flowers droop in the evening and cattle come back to their stalls, you stealthily come to my side and speak words that I do not understand.

Is this how you must woo and win me with the opiate of drowsy murmur and cold kisses, O Death, my Death?

Will there be no proud ceremony for our wedding?

Will you not tie up with a wreath your tawny coiled locks?

Is there none to carry your banner before you, and will not the night be on fire with your red torch-lights, O Death, my Death?

Come with your conch-shells sounding, come in the sleepless night.

Dress me with a crimson mantle, grasp my hand and take me.

Let your chariot be ready at my door with your horses neighing impatiently.

Raise my veil and look at my face proudly, O Death, my Death!

82

我的新娘和我,今夜要玩死亡游戏。

夜色漆黑,空中的云变幻不定,波涛在海里汹涌泡哮。

我的新娘和我,离开了睡梦的床榻,推门出去。

我们坐在秋千上,狂暴的风从身后猛烈地推着我们。

我的新娘又惊又喜,她颤抖着紧紧依偎在我的怀里。

我温柔地安慰了她好久。

我为她铺好花床,掩好房门,不让强光照到她的双眸。

我轻轻地吻她的双唇,温柔地在她耳边低语,直到她倦乏得半昏半睡。

她迷失在朦胧的无尽甜美的薄雾之中。

我爱抚她,她没有回应;我的歌唱也没能把她唤醒。

今夜,风暴的呼号从旷野飘来。

我的新娘颤抖着站起,她紧紧抓着我的手走了出来。

她的头发在风中飘扬,她的面纱浮动,她的花环在胸前瑟瑟作响。

死神的推送使她重获新生。

我的新娘和我,互相凝望,心心相印。

We are to play the game of death to-night, my bride and I.

The night is black, the clouds in the sky are capricious, and the waves are raving at sea.

We have left our bed of dreams, flung open the door and come out, my bride and I.

We sit upon a swing, and the storm winds give us a wild push from behind.

My bride starts up with fear and delight, she trembles and clings to my breast.

Long have I served her tenderly.

I made for her a bed of flowers and I closed the doors to shut out the rude light from her eyes.

I kissed her gently on her lips and whispered softly in her ears till she half swooned in languor.

She was lost in the endless mist of vague sweetness.

She answered not to my touch, my songs failed to arouse her.

Tonight has come to us the call of the storm from the wild.

My bride has shivered and stood up, she has clasped my hand and come out.

Her hair is flying in the wind, her veil is fluttering, her garland rustles over her breast.

The push of death has swung her into life.

We are face to face and heart to heart, my bride and I.

83

她住在玉米地边的山坡上,靠近那股欢笑着流经古树的庄重的阴影的清泉。女人们提着罐子到这里装水,旅客们坐在这里休息说话。她每天随着叮咚的泉韵劳作幻想。

一天晚上,一个陌生人从云中遮盖的山峰上下来;他的头发像昏昏欲睡的蛇一样纷乱纠缠。我们惊奇地问:"你是谁?"他没回答,只是坐在喧闹的泉边,默默地盯着她住的茅屋。我们吓得心咚咚乱跳。到了夜里,我们都回家去了。

第二天一早,女人们到雪松旁的泉边取水,她们发现她的茅屋的门开着,然而,她的声音没有了,她的笑脸哪去了呢?

空的水罐立在地上,她墙角的灯已经油尽火熄了。没有人知道在天亮以前她跑到哪里去了——那个陌生人也不见了。

到了五月,阳光渐强,冰雪渐融,我们坐在泉边哭泣。我们想知道:"她去的地方有泉水吗,在这燥热干渴的天气中,她能到哪里去灌满水呢?"我们沮丧地互相问:"我们住的山外还有陆地吗?"

那是一个夏天的夜里,微风从南方吹来;我坐在她的废弃的屋里,那盏熄灭的灯仍在那里立着。忽然间那座山峰,像幕帘被拉开一样从我眼前消失了。

啊，那正是她来了。"你好吗，我的孩子？你幸福吗？然而在开放的天空下，你有个躲避的地方吗？可怜啊，我们的泉水不在这里，不能缓解你的干渴了。"

"这边还是同样的天空，"她说，"只是不再受群山的遮蔽，还是同一股清泉流成了江河，还是同样的土地开阔成了平原。""一切都有了，"我叹息说，"只是我们不在。"她忧愁地笑着说："你们在我的心里。"我醒来，听见了泉流潺潺，雪松的叶子在午夜沙沙作响。

She dwelt on the hillside by the edge of a maizefield, near the spring that flows in laughing rills through the solemn shadows of ancient trees. The women came there to fill their jars, and travellers would sit there to rest and talk. She worked and dreamed daily to the tune of the bubbling stream.

One evening the stranger came down from the cloud-hidden peak; his locks were tangled like drowsy snakes. We asked in wonder, "Who are you?" He answered not but sat by the garrulous stream and silently gazed at the hut where she dwelt. Our hearts quaked in fear and we came back home when it was night.

Next morning when the women came to fetch water at the spring by the deodar trees, they found the doors open in her hut, but her voice was gone and where was her smiling face?

The empty jar lay on the floor and her lamp had burnt itself out in the corner. No one knew where she had fled to before it was morning—and the stranger had gone.

In the month of May the sun grew strong and the snow melted, and we sat by the spring and wept. We wondered in our mind, "Is there a spring in the land where she has gone and where she can fill her vessel in these hot thirsty days?" And we asked each other in dismay, "Is there a land beyond these hills where we live?"

It was a summer night; the breeze blew from the south; and I sat in her deserted room where the lamp stood still unlit. When suddenly from before my eyes the hills vanished like curtains drawn aside.

Ah, it is she who comes. How are you, my child? Are you happy? But where can you shelter under this open sky? And, alas, our spring is not here to allay your thirst."

"Here is the same sky," she said, "only free from the fencing hills, —this is the same stream grown into a river—the same earth widened into a plain." "Everything is here," I sighed, "only we are not." She smiled sadly and said, "You are in my heart." I woke up and heard the babbling of the stream and the rustling of the deodars at night.

84

　　黄绿相间的稻田上席卷过秋日的云影，后面是狂追的太阳。

　　蜜蜂为光亮而沉醉，忘了啜花蜜，傻傻地徘徊着，嗡唱着。

　　鸭子在河中的小岛上，平白无故地快乐地喧闹着。

　　都不要回家吧，兄弟们，今天早晨，都不去工作吧。

　　让我们以暴雨狂风之势占领蓝天，让我们飞奔着去掠夺空间吧。

　　笑声飘荡在空气中就好像洪水上的泡沫一样。

　　兄弟们，让我们把清晨挥霍在枉然的歌曲里吧。

Over the green and yellow rice-fields sweep the shadows of the autumn clouds followed by the swift-chasing sun.

The bees forget to sip their honey; drunken with light they foolishly hover and hum.

The ducks in the islands of the river clamour in joy for mere nothing.

Let none go back home, brothers, this morning, let none go to work.

Let us take the blue sky by storm and plunder space as we run.

Laughter floats in the air like foam on the flood.

Brothers, let us squander our morning in futile songs.

85

你是谁,读者,百年之后读着我的诗?

我不能从春天的财富里予你一朵花,也无法从天边的云彩里予你一缕金霞。

开开门向四周望望吧。

在你繁花盛放的园中,采集百年前消失了的鲜花的芬芳记忆吧。

在你心的快乐里,愿你感到一个吟唱春晨鲜活的喜悦,让它欢快的声音,穿越一百年的时光吧。

Who are you, reader, reading my poems an hundred years hence?

I cannot send you one single flower from this wealth of the spring, one single streak of gold from yonder clouds.

Open your doors and look abroad.

From your blossoming garden gather fragrant memories of the vanished flowers of an hundred years before.

In the joy of your heart may you feel the living joy that sang one spring morning, sending its glad voice across an hundred years.

FIREFLIES
流萤集

我的幻想是一群萤火虫——流光点点，闪烁在黑暗里。
My fancies are fireflies, Specks of living light twinkling in the dark.

路旁的紫罗兰吸引不住那大意的人的一瞥，它的声音只在这些零散的诗句里呢喃。
The voice of wayside pansies, that do not attract the careless glance, murmurs in these desultory lines.

在这寂静昏暗心灵的洞穴里，梦想用白天大篷车里遗落的碎片来筑造窠巢。
In the drowsy dark caves of the mind, dreams build their nest with fragments dropped from day's caravan.

春天散播花瓣，不是为了将来的果实，而是为了这一瞬间的心血来潮。
Spring scatters the petals of flowers that are not for the fruits of the future, but for the moment's whim.

从尘世睡眠中游离出来的喜悦，冲进数不尽的叶丛中，腾空飞舞，为了一日之愉。
Joy freed from the bond of earth's slumber rushes into numberless leaves, and dances in the air for a day.

我的话语轻微，但当我的作品意味深重而沉淀时，它们却能在时光的浪头上翩翩起舞。
My words that are slight may lightly dance upon time's waves when my works heavy with import have gone down.

心底的飞蛾长着纤薄的翅翼，在日落的天空作别离的飞翔。
Mind's underground moths grow filmy wings and take a farewell flight in the sunset sky.

蝴蝶细数的不是月份,而是瞬间,
她拥有富足的光阴。
*The butterfly counts not months but moments,
and has time enough.*

我的心思像星火,带着淳朴的欢笑,骑着惊奇的翅膀飞走了。
*My thoughts, like sparks, ride on winged surprises,
carrying a single laughter.*

那树深情地凝望着它绮丽的倩影,可是永远捉不到它。
*The tree gazes in love at its own beautiful shadow
which yet it never can grasp.*

让我的爱宛若日光一般地环绕你,并给你绚烂的自由。
*Let my love, like sunlight, surround you and yet give
you illumined freedom.*

白天是色彩斑斓的泡沫,浮动在高深莫测的夜的表面上。
*Days are coloured bubbles that float upon the surface
of fathomless night.*

我的奉献羞怯得不能要求你纪念,因此你也许会铭记它们。
My offerings are too timid to claim your remembrance, and therefore you may remember them.

如果我的名字是一种累赘,从这礼物上略去它吧,但请保留我的诗歌。
Leave out my name from the gift if it be a burden, but keep my song.

四月,像个小孩,用花朵把象形文字写在尘土中,又把它拂去,就此忘却。
April, like a child, writes hieroglyphs on dust with flowers, wipes them away and forgets.

记忆,这女祭司,残害了现在,又把它的心奉献给了那已死去的过去。
Memory, the priestess, kill the present and offers its heart to the shrine of the dead past.

从那庄重晦暗的寺庙里,小孩们跑出来坐在尘土里,上帝看着他们游戏却忘却了那位祭司。
From the solemn gloom of the temple children run out to sit in the dust, God watchs them play and forgets the priest.

我的心在思想之流里因瞬间的闪亮而开始活跃,宛若小溪因它自己突然灵动的永不重复的音符而流转一般。
My mind starts up at some flash on the flow of its thoughts like a brook at a sudden liquid note of its own that is never repeated.

山上,寂静涌起,探索它自己的高峻;湖里,波澜止息,静想它自己的深邃。
In the mountain, stillness surges up to explore its own height; in the lake, movement stands still to contemplate its own depth.

即将离开的夜在清晨闭着的眼睛上留下一吻,成为星辰中的光亮。
The departing night's one kiss on the closed eyes of morning glows in the star of dawn.

少女啊,你的美像一颗尚未成熟的果实,紧紧地藏着一个不肯吐露的秘密。
Maiden, thy beauty is like a fruit which is yet to mature, tense with an unyielding secret.

失去了记忆的哀愁像沙哑晦暗的光阴,没有鸟儿的歌唱,只有那蟋蟀的唧唧声。
Sorrow that has lost its memory is like the dumb dark hours that have no bird songs but only the cricket's chirp.

偏执想把真理稳妥地抓在手里,却牢牢地捏死了它。广袤的夜空想振奋一盏畏怯的灯,就点起了她所有璀璨的繁星。
Bigotry tries to keep truth safe in its hand with a grip that kill it. Wishing to hearten a timid lamp, great night lights all her stars.

天空虽然想把大地新娘拥进臂弯,却仍旧无限遥远。
Though he holds in his arms the earth-bride, the sky is ever immensely away.

上帝寻求同伴并要求爱,魔鬼寻求奴隶并要求顺从。
God seeks comrades and claims love, the Devil seeks slaves and claims obedience.

泥土把树木绑缚在她身上作为她服务的回报，天空却什么也不要，就让它自由生长。
The soil in return for her service keeps the tree tied to her, the sky asks nothing and leaves it free.

宛若仙子的宝石，并不吹嘘它年代的悠久，而是为那瞬间的闪烁而自豪。
Jewellike the immortal does not boast of its length of years but of the scintillating point of its moment.

小孩永远住在永恒的时间的玄妙里,不会被历史的尘埃埋浸。
The child ever dwells in the mystery of ageless time, unobscured by the dust of history.

在创造的脚步里轻盈的一笑,快速地飞过了时光之流。
A light laughter in the steps of creation carries it swiftly across time.

那个离我遥远的人在清晨就走近了我,并且当他被黑夜带走时,却更靠近我。
One who was distant came near to me in the morning, and still nearer when taken away by night.

粉色和白色的夹竹桃萍水相逢,用不同的方言说笑快活。
White and pink oleanders meet and make merry in different dialects.

平和在积极地清扫它的灰尘时,它就是风暴。
When peace is active sweeping its dirt, it is storm.

湖泊低躺在山脚下,像在僵硬的人的脚边含泪乞求爱。
The lake lies low by the hill, a tearful entreaty of love at the foot of the inflexible.

那圣洁的孩子微笑着,在他那无意义的云层和短暂的光与影的玩具中嬉戏。
There smiles the Divine Child among his playthings of unmeaning clouds and ephemeral lights and shadows.

微风对荷花低声耳语:"你的秘密是什么?"
荷花答:"是我自己,你把它窃走吧,那我也就消失了!"
The breeze whispers to the lotus," what is thy secret?"
"It is myself," says the lotus," steal it and I disapper!"

暴风雨的自由和树干的束缚,在摇曳的枝干中手舞足蹈。
The freedom of the storm and the bondage of the stem join hands in the dance of swaying branches.

茉莉对太阳情意绵绵的呢喃就是她的花朵。
The jasmine's lisping of love to the sun is her flowers.

暴君要求放手地残害自由,却还要把自由占为己有。
The tyrant claims freedom to kill freedom and yet to keep it for himself.

天神厌烦了他们的天堂,就羡慕人了。
Gods, tired of their paradise, envy man.

云就是烟雾之山,山就是乱石之云,——这就是时光之梦里的幻想曲。
Clouds are hills in vapour, hills are clouds in stone, —a phantasy in time's dream.

上帝等着人们用爱去筑成他的圣庙,人们却带来了石头。
While God waits for His temple to be built of love, men bring stones.

我在自己的歌里触摸到上帝,犹如高山用它的瀑布触摸到遥远的海洋。
I touch God in my song as the hill touches the far-away sea with its waterfall.

光从云朵的抗衡里发现了她色彩缤纷的珍宝。
Light finds her treasure of colours through the antagonism of clouds.

我今日之心对它哭泣的昨夜微笑，宛若一棵潮湿的树在雨后的阳光中熠熠生辉。
My heart to-day smiles at its past night of tears like a wet tree glistening in the sun after the rain is over.

我感谢过了那使我生命结出果实的树木，但不曾记起那使我生命常青的小草。
I have thanked the trees that have made my life fruitful, but have failed to remember the grass that has ever kept it green.

独一无二只是虚幻，并蒂齐放才使它真实。
The one without second is emptiness, the other one makes it true.

生命中许多过错哭求仁慈的美来调和他们的孤立，为了与整体相和谐。
Life's errors cry for the merciful beauty that can modulate their isolation into a harmony with the whole.

他们期盼那放逐了的窝巢的感激，因为他们的笼子美观且牢固。
They expect thanks for the banished nest because their cage is shapely and secure.

不论你是什么，在爱情里，我会偿还你无穷的相思债。
In love I pay my endless debt to thee for what thou art.

在百合花丛中，池塘从幽暗处献上了它的抒情诗，太阳称赞他们很好。
The pond sends up its lyrics from its dark in lilies, and the sun says, they are good.

你对伟大者的诽谤是不虔敬，它只会伤到你自己；你对渺小者的诽谤是卑劣，因为它伤害了受害者。
Your calumny against the great is impious, it hurts yourself; against the small it is mean, for it hurts the victim.

这地上绽放的第一朵花是对那未来的歌的邀请。
The first flower that blossomed on this earth was an invitation to the unborn song.

黎明——这五彩斑斓的花——凋零了,于是那纯朴的光之果实,那太阳就冉冉升起了。
Dawn—the many—coloured flower—fades, and then simple light fruit, the sun appears.

肌肉怀疑它的智慧掐死了声音不让它哭喊。
The muscle that has a doubt of its wisdom throttles the voice that would cry.

风儿试图用风暴掠夺火焰,却把它吹灭了。
The wind tries to take the flame by storm only to blow it out.

生命的游戏转瞬结束，生命的玩具一件件被遗弃在后面，然后被忘却。
Life's play is swift, Life's playthings fall behind one by one and are forgotten.

我的花啊，不要在傻瓜的扣眼里找寻你的天堂。
My flower, seek not thy paradise in a fool's buttonhole.

我的新月，你起来晚了，但是我的夜莺还保持清醒来与你打招呼。
Thou hast risen late, my crescent moon, but my night bird is still awake to greet thee.

黑夜是遮了面纱的新娘沉静地期望着那流转的光重回到她怀抱。
Darkness is the veiled bride silently waiting for the errant light to return to her bosom.

树木是大地对聆听的天空不停地无止境的倾诉。
Trees are the earth's endless effort to speak to the listening heaven.

我嘲笑自己时,自我的重担就减轻了。
The burden of self is lightened when I laugh at myself.

弱者也可能是令人畏惧的,因为他们奋力地想表现得强大。
The weak can be terrible because they try furiously to appear strong.

天堂的风吹起,船锚死命地抓住泥浆,我的小船就用胸膛紧偎着锚链。
The wind of heaven blows, the anchor desperately clutches the mud, and my boat is beating its breast against the chain.

死的精髓是归一，生的精髓是众多。当上帝死去时，宗教便会合而为一了。
The spirit of death is one, the spirit of life is many. When God is dead religion becomes one.

天空的蔚蓝渴望着大地的碧绿，风儿在天地间叹气："唉！"
The blue of the sky longs for the earth's green, the wind between them sighs, "Alas."

白天的苦痛被它自己的强光遮蔽了，夜晚却在群星中灼烧起来。
Day's pain muffled by its own glare, burns among stars in the night.

群星拥在童贞的夜晚，敬畏地对着她那永难触及的孤寂。
The stars crowd round the virgin night in silent awe at her loneliness that can never be touched.

云彩把它全部的黄金倾洒给即将别离的太阳，只用一抹苍白的微笑招呼初升的月亮。
The cloud gives all its gold to the departing sun and greets the rising moon with only a pale smile.

行善者来到庙门口，博爱者走进圣殿。
He who does good comes to the temple gate, he who loves reaches the shrine.

花儿啊，怜悯这小虫吧，它不是蜜蜂，它的爱只是一种过错和累赘。
Flower, have pity for the worm, it is not a bee, its love is a blunder and burden.

孩子们用恐怖的胜利的废墟建起他们洋娃娃的房子。
With the ruins of terror's triumph children build their doll's house.

灯盏在冷漠而漫长的白天里等候夜晚光焰的亲吻。
The lamp waits through the long day of neglect for the flame's kiss in the night.

羽毛懒洋洋而知足地躺在尘埃里,忘却了自己的天空。
Feathers in the dust lying lazily content have forgotten their sky.

孤苦伶仃的花儿不必羡妒遍地的荆棘。
The flower which is single need not envy the thorns that are numerous.

世界在其善意者的无私暴政下而承受着极大的苦痛。
The world suffers most from the disinterested tyranny of its well-wisher.

当我们为生存权利付出了至高的代价后才赢得自由。
We gain freedom when we have paid the full price for our right to live.

你这一瞬间漫不经心的礼物竟像秋夜的流星,在我生命的深处燃起了火。

Your careless gifts of a moment, like the meteors of an autumn night, catch fire in the depth of my being.

在种子的心中等候的信仰承诺一个它不能立刻证明的生命的奇迹。

The faith waiting in the heart of a seed promises a miracle of life which it cannot prove at once.

春天在寒冬的门前踌躇，但芒果花贸然地奔向他，在她花期之前，便突遭了她的厄运。
Spring hesitates at winter's door, but the mango blossom rashly runs out to him before her time and meets her doom.

世界是不断变化的浮沫漂在静默之海面上。
The world is the ever-changing foam that floats on the surface of a sea of silence.

两个遥遥相望的海岸在深不可测的泪海之歌里融入它们的呼喊。
The two separated shores mingle their voices in a song of unfathomed tears.

如同江河流进沧海,劳作在闲暇的深处觅到了完满。
As a river in the sea, work finds its fulfilment in the depth of leisure.

我在路上踌躇,直到你的樱花纷纷凋零,但我的爱人呀,杜鹃花却把你的宽恕带给我。
I lingered on my way till thy cherry tree lost its blossom, but the azalea brings to me, my love, thy forgiveness.

今天,你害羞的小石榴花蕾,在她面纱后面红着脸,明天当我离去后,却会绽放热情的花朵。
Thy shy little pomegranate bud, blushing to-day behind her veil, will burst into a passionate flower to-morrow when I am away.

粗笨的蛮力弄坏了锁匙,只好使用铁镐。
The clumsiness of power spoils the key, and uses the pickaxe.

新生是从夜晚的神秘进入白天更大的神秘里。
Brith is from the mystery of night into the greater mystery of day.

我的这些纸船意图在时光的涟漪上跳舞,却不想要抵达任何目的地。
These paper boats of mine are meant to dance on the ripples of hours, and not to reach any destination.

流离的歌儿从我心中飞出，在你爱的呼唤里寻觅窝巢。
Migratory songs wing from my heart and seek their nests in your voice of love.

危险，猜疑，和拒绝的汪洋环绕着人们的确定的小岛，让他向未知发起挑战。
The sea of danger, doubt and denial around man's little island of certainty challenges him to dare the unknown.

爱情宽恕时便是惩戒，受到伤害的美用可怕的沉默来惩罚。
Love punishes when it forgives, and injured beauty by its awful silence.

你孤独地活着，从未有回报，因为他们畏惧你极大的价值。
You live alone and unrecompensed because they are afraid of your great worth.

在一串无穷的黎明中，同一个太阳刚刚从新土地里重生。
The same sun is newly born in new lands in a ring of endless dawns.

上帝的世界永远在死亡里重生，魔鬼的世界却总被它自身的存在所粉碎。
God's world is ever renewed by death, a Titan's ever crushed by its own existence.

萤火虫在尘埃中探索时，从来不知道有漫天的繁星。
The glow-worm while exploring the dust never knows that stars are in the sky.

树木是今天的，花儿却是昔日的，她带来太古时种子的讯息。
The tree is of to-day, the flower is old, it brings with it the message of the immemorial seed.

每一朵盛放的玫瑰都给我从永恒的春天之"玫瑰"带来问候。
Each rose that comes brings me greetings from the Rose of an eternal spring.

我劳作时，上帝就给我赞誉，我歌唱时他就予我爱恋。
God honours me when I work, He loves me when I sing.

在昨天的爱遗弃的巢里,我今天的爱无家可归。
My love of to-day finds no home in the nest deserted by yesterday's love.

苦痛的火透过她的哀愁为我心灵探寻到一条光明之径。
The fire of pain traces for my soul a luminous path across her sorrow.

草儿从数不尽的死亡中重生,所以山丘消失后它依然存在。
The grass survives the hill through its resurrections from countless deaths.

你从我手中猛然消失了,只在蔚蓝的天空里留下了无从感觉的轻抚,摇曳在风里,浮晃在阴影里,无法看见的幻影。

Thou hast vanished from my reach leaving an impalpable touch in the blue of the sky, an invisible image in the wind moving among the shadows.

为了悲悯那萧条的树枝,春天留给它一个在孤叶上颤抖的亲吻。

In pity for the desolate branch spring leaves to it a kiss that fluttered in a lonely leaf.

花园里的阴影静默地爱恋着太阳,花儿猜到了这秘密,就莞尔一笑,而树叶却窃窃私语。

The shy shadow in the garden loves the sun in silence, Flowers guess the secret, and smile, while the leaves whisper.

我没有在天空留下翅膀的痕迹,但我已飞过,心中满是欣喜。
I leave no trace of wings in the air, but I am glad I have had my flight.

萤火虫在草叶丛中闪烁,使得繁星都惊叹不已。
The fireflies, twinkling among leaves, make the stars wonder.

山仿佛被云雾打败,却始终毫不动摇。
The mountain remains unmoved at its seeming defeat by the mist.

当玫瑰对太阳说"我将永远记住你",她的花瓣就飘落到尘埃里。
While the rose said to the sun, "I shall ever remember thee,"her petals fell to the dust.

山岳是大地向那难以企及的青天所表现出的绝望姿态。
Hills are the earth's gesture of despair for the unreachable.

虽然那花间的刺扎痛了我,美啊,我仍然感激。
Though the thorn in thy flower pricked me, O Beauty, I am grateful.

世人知道，少数多过多数。
The world knows that the few are more than the many.

朋友，别让我的爱成为你的累赘，要明白它自己就是回报。
Let not my love be a burden on you, my friend, know that it pays itself.

黎明在黑暗的门前弹着她的琵琶，当太阳出来时她便心甘情愿地消隐。
Dawn plays her lute before the gate of darkness, and is content to vanish when the sun comes out.

美即是真理的微笑，当她在一面完美的镜子面前看到自己的面庞时。
Beauty is truth's smile when she beholds her own face in a perfect mirror.

露珠对太阳的认识只在它自己的微小的球体里。
The dewdrop knows the sun only within its own tiny orb.

绝望的思想，从历代被抛弃了的蜂巢里飞出，蜂拥至天空，围绕我心头嗡嗡低吟，并寻找我的声音。
Forlorn thoughts from the forsaken hives of all ages, swarming in the air, hum round my heart and seek my voice.

沙漠被监禁在它自己的无限贫瘠的沙墙里。
The desert is imprisoned the wall of its unbounded barrenness.

在细叶的轻颤中我看到了空气无形的舞蹈，还在它们若隐若现的微光里看到了天空隐秘的心跳。
In the thrill of little leaves I see the air's invisible dance, and in their glimmering the secret heart-beats of the sky.

你就像一棵开满花的树，当我颂扬你的天赋时使你诧异。
You are like a flowering tree, amazed when I praise you for your gifts.

大地的祭火在她的树林里燃起热焰，把火花散射到花丛中。
The earth's sacrificial fire flames up in her trees, scattering sparks in flowers.

森林，这大地之云，把它们的沉静贡献给天空，云就从上面降落像共鸣的骤雨。
Forests, the clouds of earth, hold up to the sky their silence, and clouds from above come down in resonant showers.

世界用图像和我说话,我的灵魂以音乐作答。
The world speaks to me in pictures, my soul answers in music.

天空整晚对它的露珠谈着数不尽的星星,以此怀念太阳。
The sky tells its beads all night on the countless stars in memory of the sun.

夜的黑暗,像苦痛一样,是麻木的,黎明的黑暗,像和平一样,是沉静的。
The darkness of night, like pain ,is dumb ,the darkness of dawn, like peace, is silent.

自豪在石头上雕下他的蹙眉,爱情在花朵上献出她的屈服。
Pride engraves his frowns in stones, love offers her surrender in flowers.

献媚的画笔遵从狭隘的画布把真理缩减了。
The obsequious brush curtails truth in deference to the canvas which is narrow.

小山丘倾慕遥远的天空时,愿像云朵一般无止尽地寻求。
The hill in its longing for the far-away sky wishes to be like the cloud with its endless urge of seeking.

为了要证明他们洒墨是正确的,他们把白天改写成了黑夜。
To justify their own spilling of ink they spell the day as night.

当善良有利可图之时，利益就对善良微笑了。
Profit smiles on goodness when the good is profitable.

在膨胀的傲慢中，泡沫质疑大海的真实性，狂妄一笑，就爆裂成虚无。
In its swelling pride the bubble doubts the truth of the sea, and laughs and bursts into emptiness.

爱情是一种无止境的神秘，因为没有别的什么可以诠释它。
Love is an endless mystery, for it has nothing else to explain it.

我的云朵，在黑暗中哀愁，忘却了它们自己已经遮掩了太阳。
My clouds, sorrowing in the dark, forget that they themselves have hidden the sun.

当上帝来向他们索要礼物之时，人们才发现了自己的财富。
Man discovers his own wealth when God comes to ask gifts of him.

你将记忆当作火焰留在我孤独的别离之灯里。
You leave your memory as a flame to my lonely lamp of separation.

我来献给你一朵鲜花,而你却一定要拥有我的整座花园,它都是你的了。
I came to offer thee a flower, but thou must have all my garden, it is thine.

这幅图画——光明之记忆被暗影珍藏着。
The picture—a memory of light treasured by the shadow.

冲着太阳做鬼脸是容易的,从任何方面看,他都裸露在自己的光亮里。
It is easy to make faces at the sun, he is exposed by his own light in all directions.

爱情即使说出口仍然是个秘密,因为只有爱人才真正明白他是被爱着的。
Love remains a secret even when spoken, for only a lover truly knows that he is loved.

历史缓慢地窒息了它的真理,但又急忙地在极度的苦痛中忏悔,拼命令它复活。
History slowly smothers its truth, but hastily struggles to revive it in the terrible penance of pain.

我的工作只有每天的薪水作为回报,我却在爱里等候我最终的价值。
My work is rewarded in daily wages, I wait for my final value in love.

美晓得说"足够了",野蛮却叫嚣着要索求更多。
Beauty knows to say: "Enough," barbarism clamours for still more.

上帝不愿意看到我做他的奴仆，而是替众生服务的上帝自己。
God loves to see in me, not his servant, but himself who serves all.

夜的黑暗与白天是和谐的，烟雾蔼蔼的早晨却和它不搭调。
The darkness of night is in harmony with day, the morning of mist is discordant.

在玫瑰怒放的时节里,爱情是佳酿,但当花瓣凋零的时候,它就是充饥的食粮了。
In the bounteous time of roses love is wine,— it is food in the famished hour when their petals are shed.

在异乡一朵无名的花对那诗人说:"我的爱人啊,我们不是在同一片乡土中生活吗?"
An unknown flower in a strange land speaks to the poet: "Are we not of the same soil, my lover?"

我能爱我的上帝,因为他给了我否定他的自由。
I am able to love my God because he gives me freedom to deny him.

我那没调好的琴弦在它们羞愧的苦涩哭喊中乞求音乐。
My untuned strings beg for music in their anguished cry of shame.

书虫觉得人类不吃书是异乎寻常和非常痴笨的。
The worm thinks it strange and foolish that man does not eat his books.

今天乌云密布的天空在永恒深思的前额上，展现了天生哀愁暗影的幻象。
The clouded sky today bears the vision of the shadow of a divine sadness on the forehead of brooding eternity.

我的树荫是为了路过的人们,它的果实是为了我所等候的那个人。
The shade of my tree is for passers-by, its fruit for the one for whom I wait.

地球让落日的余晖给晕红了脸,宛若一只熟透的果实,准备让夜晚来收获。
Flushed with the glow of sunset earth seems like a ripe fruit ready to be harvested by night.

为了创造光明的缘故,光明接受了黑暗做配偶。
Light accepts darkness for his spouse for the sake of creation.

芦苇等候他主人的气息,而"主人"却在找寻他的芦苇。
The reed waits for his master's breath, the Master goes seeking for his reed.

在那盲目的笔看来,写字的手是虚幻的,它所写的完全没有意义。
To the blind pen the hand that writes is unreal, its writing unmeaning.

大海重击他贫瘠的胸膛,因为他没有鲜花献给月亮。
The sea smites his own barren breast because he has no flowers to offer to the moon.

贪心果子的,失去了花卉。
The greed for fruit misses the flower.

上帝在他繁星满缀的庙宇里等候人们带给他灯火。
God in His temple of stars waits for man to bring him his lamp.

束缚在树里的火幻化成了花朵,从牢笼中释放出来,那厚颜无耻的火焰死在荒芜的余烬中。
The fire restrained in the tree fashions flowers. Released from bonds, the shameless flame dies in barren ashes.

天空并没有设下圈套去俘虏月亮,只是她自己的自由绑缚了她。
The sky sets no snare to capture the moon, it is her own freedom which binds her.

盈满天空的光亮,在草上的露珠里探求自己的极限。
The light that fills the sky seeks its limit in a dew-drop on the grass.

财富是沉重的负累,幸福是生命的完满。
Wealth is the burden of bigness, Welfare the fulness of being.

当剃刀嘲笑太阳时,它以自己的刀口锋利得意。
The razor-blade is proud of its keenness when is sneers at the sun.

蝴蝶有闲空去爱慕荷花,忙于储蜜的蜂儿却没有这等闲空。
The butterfly has leisure to love the lotus, not the bee busily storing honey.

孩子，你装进我心坎里的，是那风和海水潺潺相激之声，花朵默然的秘密，云儿的幻梦，和晨空哑然的凝视。
Child, thou bring to my heart the babble of the wind and the water, the flowers' speechless secrets, the clouds' dreams, the mute gaze of wonder of the morning sky.

云里的彩虹也许是绮丽的，但灌木丛中的小蝴蝶更美妙动人。
The rainbow among the clouds may be great but the little butterfly among the bushes is greater.

薄雾织网来笼罩早晨，使他着迷，让他盲目。
The mist weaves her net round the morning, captivates him, and makes him blind.

晨星对黎明低语道:"告诉我你仅仅是为了我而存在的。"
她回答道:"是的,我也是仅仅为了那不知名的花朵而存在的。"
The Morning Star whispers to Dawn, "Tell me that you are only for me."
"Yes, "she answers," And also only for that nameless flower."

天空为大地保持无尽的空间,让她用梦想在那儿筑造自己的天堂。
The sky remains infinitely vacant for earth there to build its heaven with dreams.

当新月被告知它只是一片等候完美的碎片时,也许会疑惑地微笑。
Perhaps the crescent moon smiles in doubt at being told that it is a fragment awaiting perfection.

让黄昏饶恕白天的过错吧,并因此为自己赢得安宁。
Let the evening forgive the mistakes of the day and thus win peace for herself.

在花蕾的囚笼里，在甜蜜的不完美的心里，
美丽莞尔一笑。
*Beauty smiles in the confinement of the bud,
in the heart of a sweet incompleteness.*

你飘忽不定的爱情用翅膀轻拂我的向日葵，从来没有问过它是否已准备好奉献它的花蜜。
*Your flitting love lightly brushed with its
wings my sun-flower and never asked if it was
ready to surrender its honey.*

叶子是静默地拥着花朵——每朵花都是叶子的语言。
*Leaves are silences around flowers which are
their words.*

树木背负着它的千年的岁月，宛若壮丽庄严的瞬间。
*The tree bears its thousand years as one large
majestic moment.*

我的供品不是给路尽头的庙宇,而是给路边的神龛,每一次转弯时它们都令我惊异。
My offerings are not for the temple at the end of the road, but for the wayside shrines that surprise me at every bend.

我的爱,你的微笑宛若一朵奇特的花,纯洁简单而让人捉摸不透。
Your smile. my love, like the smile of a strange flower, is simple and inexplicable.

当死者的功绩被夸大时,死神狂笑,因为这已超过他自称的功绩,他的仓库已经容纳不下了。
Death laughs when the merit of the dead is exaggerated for it swells his store with more than he can claim.

海岸的叹息徒劳地追随催促大船赶忙飘过海洋的微风。
The sigh of the shore follows in vain the breeze that hastens the ship across the sea.

真理热爱自己的穷尽,因为它在那里偶遇美丽。
Truth loves its limits, for there it meets the beautiful.

我和你分隔的两岸之间,有一片浩瀚的海洋,那是波涛滂沛的自我,我渴求横渡它。
Between the shores of Me and Thee there is the loud ocean, my own surging self, which I long to cross.

占有权愚笨地吹嘘它的享有权。
The right to possess boasts foolishly of its right to enjoy.

玫瑰不只是为了它的刺而羞赧地致歉。
The rose is a great deal more than a blushing apology for the thorn.

白天把他的金琵琶献给繁星的静谧，去为了无穷的生命而调弦。
Day offers to the silence of stars his golden lute to be tuned for the endless life.

智者知道怎样教育，愚者知道怎样鞭打。
The wise know how to teach, the fool how to smite.

在永存的圆舞中，圆心静止而沉默。
The centre is still and silent in the heart of an eternal dance of circles.

裁判员认为自己是公正的，当他拿别人的灯油和自己的灯光相比时。
The judge thinks that he is just when he compares the oil of another's lamp with the light of his own.

被俘获的花儿在国王的花环上苦笑，当草地上的野花在倾慕她的时候。

The captive flower in the King's wreath smiles bitterly when the meadow-flower envies her.

山峦的积雪是自己的负累，它倾注出来的溪流却由全世界来背负。

Its store of snow is the hill's own burden, its outpouring of streams is borne by all the world.

请听森林为他的花朵能自由绽放而祈祷。

Listen to the prayer of the forest for its freedom in flowers.

让你的爱情看见我吧，即使隔着一层亲近的屏障。

Let your love see me even through the barrier of nearness.

在创作中，工作的劲头会带动并且助长游戏的兴致。

The spirit of work in creation is there to carry and help the spirit of play.

背着乐器的重负，计算它的物质成本，而从来不知道那是用于音乐演奏的东西，这就是耳聋生命的不幸。
To carry the burden of the instrument, count the cost of its material, and never to know that it is for music, is the tragedy of deaf life.

信仰是能感知光亮的鸟儿，当黎明还阴暗时就唱起歌来了。
Faith is the bird that feels the light and sings when the dawn is still dark.

夜啊，我带给你，我白天的空杯子，为了新的一天的晨宴，请用你清爽的黑暗涤荡它。
I bring to thee, night, my day's empty cup, to be cleansed with thy cool darkness for a new morning's festival.

山上的冷杉沙沙作响，把它与风暴对抗的往事调制成平和的圣诗。
The mountain fir, in its rustling, modulates the memory of its fights with the storm into a hymn of peace.

当我叛逆之时,上帝用他的抗争成就了我;当我疲惫之时,他无视我。
God honoured me with his fight when I was rebellious, He ignored me when I was languid.

宗派主义者认为他已经把海水都舀进了他私人的池塘里了。
The sectarian thinks that he has the sea ladled into his private pond.

在生命的背阴深处,有很多寂寞的无须赘言的回忆之巢。
In the shady depth of life are the lonely nests of memories that shrink from words.

让我的爱在白天的劳动里获得力量，在夜晚的结合中得到安宁吧。
Let my love find its strength in the service of day, its peace in the union of night.

生命在草叶里向不知名的光亮呈献它沉默的圣诗。
Life sends up in blades of grass its silent hymn of praise to the unnamed Light.

夜晚的星星对我而言，是我白天凋零的花朵的追忆悼念。
The stars of night are to me the memorials of my day's faded flowers.

打开你的门，让那一定要走的走吧，因为阻拦会让失去变得很不得体。
Open thy door to that which must go, for the loss becomes unseemly when obstructed.

真正的完结不在于达到某种极限，而在于永无止境地完成。
True end is not in the reaching of the limit, but in a completion which is limitless.

海岸对大海低语道:"将你的波浪竭力想说的写给我吧。"
大海就用泡沫写了又写,但在哄然的绝望里擦除了一行行的字。
The shore whispers to the sea: "Write to me what thy waves struggle to say."
The sea writes in foam again and again and wipes off the lines in a boisterous despair.

让你手指轻拨我的生命之弦,奏出属于你和我的音乐。
Let the touch of thy finger thrill my life's strings and make the music thine and mine.

内在的世界好似果实环伏在我生命里,在喜悦和哀愁中成熟,它将掉进原本的泥土的黑暗里去,为了更深层次的创造。
The inner world rounded in my life like a fruit, matured in joy and sorrow, will drop into the darkness of the original soil for some further course of creation.

形式在"物"中,旋律在"力"中,意义在"人"中。
Form is in Matter, rhythm in Force, meaning in the Person.

有人寻求智慧，也有人寻求财富，我只寻求与你相伴，
好让我唱歌。
*There are seekers of wisdom and seekers of wealth, I
seek thy company so that I may sing.*

宛若树木的落叶，我将语言撒在地上，让我的思想在你
的静默里落下无言的花朵吧。
*As the tree its leaves, I shed my words on the earth, let
my thoughts unuttered flower in thy silence.*

主啊，我对真理的信仰，我对完美的理解，帮助你的创造。
*My faith in truth, my vision of the perfect, help thee,
Master, in thy creation.*

我全部的喜悦来自于生命的果实和花朵,盛宴结束之时,让我献给你完满和谐的爱意。
All the delights that I have felt in life's fruits and flowers, let me offer to thee at the end of the feast, in a perfect union of love.

有些人深谋远虑,探寻你的真理的意味,他们很伟大;我只会聆听追随你弹奏的音乐,我很快乐。
Some have thought deeply and explored the meaning of thy truth, and they are great; I have listened to catch the music of thy play, and I am glad.

树木是带翼的精灵,挣脱了种子的束缚,在未知的世界里追寻生命的冒险。
The tree is a winged spirit released from the bondage of seed, pursuing its adventure of life across the unknown.

荷花把它的美丽献给天堂,绿草却把它奉献给大地。
The lotus offers its beauty to the heaven, the grass its service to the earth.

太阳的亲吻使依偎在枝干的青涩的果实因为丢弃吝啬而成熟。
The sun's kiss mellows into abandonment, the miserliness of the green fruit clinging to its stem.

火焰和我心里的瓦灯相逢,多么令人赞叹的光亮啊!
The flame met the earthen lamp in me, and what a great marvel of light!

谬误往往和真理毗邻,因此常常蛊惑我们。
Mistakes live in the neighbourhood of truth and therefore delude us.

乌云嗤笑彩虹,说它只是华而不实暴发的绮丽,彩虹镇静地回答:"我和太阳本身一样的真实。"

The cloud laughed at the rainbow saying that it was an upstart gaudy in its emptiness. The rainbow calmly answered, "I am as inevitably real as the sun himself."

不要让我在黑暗里徒劳摸索,让我头脑保持镇静地深信白天必将来临,真理也必将出现在它的简单里。

Let me not grope in vain in the dark but keep my mind still in the faith that the day will break and truth will appear in its simplicity.

穿过寂静的黑夜,我听到早晨飘荡的希望归来了,敲击着我的心。

Through the silent night I hear the returning vagrant hopes of the morning knock at my heart.

我新的爱人来了，带给我古老而永久的财富。
My new love comes bringing to me the eternal wealth of the old.

大地凝望着月亮，惊异她竟然将全部的音乐融进笑容里了。
The earth gazes at the moon and wonders that she should have all her music in her smile.

白天用好奇的、耀眼的目光把星星吓飞了。
Day with its glare of curiosity puts the stars to flight.

天空啊，我的心和你真的合而为一了，就在我自己的窗边，而不是在旷野里，那边是你独占的王国。
My mind has its true union with thee, O sky, at the window which is mine own, and not in the open where thou hast thy sole kingdom.

人们把上帝的花称作自己的,且他把它们织成了花环。
Man claims God's flowers as his own when he weaves them in a garland.

被埋葬了的城市,赤裸裸地暴露到一个崭新时代的阳光下,却为丧失了所有的歌而羞愧。
The buried city, laid bare to the sun of a new age, is ashamed that it has lost all its songs.

就像那早已没有意义的我的心痛,披着黑暗霓裳的日光,把他们自己隐藏在地下,就像爱情突然触动的我的心痛,他们应春天的呼唤而摘下面纱,在五彩缤纷的红花绿叶的狂欢中走出来。

Like my heart's pain that has long missed its meaning, the sun's rays robed in dark hide themselves under the ground. Like my heart's pain at love's sudden touch, they change their veil at the spring's call and come out in the carnival of colours, in flowers and leaves.

我生命的空洞的玉笛等候它最终的音乐,像繁星出来之前原始的黑暗。
My life's empty flute waits for its final music like the primal darkness before the stars came out.

从泥土的束缚中挣脱出来,对于树木而言并非自由。
Emancipation from the bondage of the soil is no freedom for the tree.

人生故事的绣帷,是用生命结上的细线编织成的,永远在织了又拆,拆了又织。
The tapestry of life's story is woven with the threads of life's ties ever joining and breaking.

我那些从来没有被语言捕获到的思想栖于我的歌舞中。
The thoughts of mine that are never captured by words perch upon my songs and dance.

今晚我的灵魂迷失在一株孤独的树的心里，那株树寂寞地在无限的低语中。
My soul tonight loses itself in the silent heart of a tree standing alone among the whispers of immensity.

珍珠贝壳被大海抛到了死亡沙滩，这是对于创造生命的极大浪费。
Pearl shells cast up by the sea on death's barren beach, a magnificent wastefulness of creative life.

太阳的光为我开启了世界之门，爱的光为我开启了世界的珍宝。
The sunlight opens for me the world's gate, love's light its treasure.

我的生命就像多节的芦笛，穿过它希望和收获的缝隙，便奏出多彩的音乐。
My life like the reed with its stops, has its play of colours through the gaps in its hopes and gains.

别让我对你的感谢,从我的静默中夺去更多的尊重。
Let not my thanks to thee rob my silence of its fuller homage.

生命的憧憬到来时,总伪装成小孩子。
Life's aspirations come in the guise of children.

凋零的花朵哀叹道,春天已经永远消逝了。
The faded flower sighs that the spring has vanished for ever.

在我生命的花园里,我的财富总是光亮和阴影,从来就没有被收集和储藏过。
In my life's garden my wealth has been of the shadows and lights that are never gathered and stored.

我一直以来收获的果实,就是你所接受的那颗。
The fruit that I have gained for ever is that which thou hast accepted.

茉莉花知道太阳是她天堂的兄弟。
The jasmine knows the sun to be her brother in the heaven.

光是古老而年轻的,影是瞬息的,出生就老了。
Light is young, the ancient light, shadows are of the moment, they are born old.

我感觉到,到白天的尽头,我的歌声将渡我到彼岸,在那儿我会看得清楚。
I feel that the ferry of my songs at the day's end will bring me across to the other shore from where I shall see.

那只在花丛间飞来飞去的蝴蝶永远是属于我的,我却丢掉了网住的那只。
The butterfly flitting from flower to flower ever remains mine, I lose the one that is netted by me.

自由的鸟儿，你的歌声飘进了我的睡巢，而我倦怠的羽翼却梦想游历到云朵之上的光明中。
Your voice, free bird, reaches my sleeping nest, and my drowsy wings dream of a voyage to the light above the clouds.

我不明白在人生的戏剧中我所饰演的角色有什么意义，因为我对别人饰演的角色也是一概不知。
I miss the meaning of my own part in the play of life because I know not of the parts that others play.

花儿落尽了所有的花瓣，就获得了果实。
The flower sheds all its petals and finds the fruit.

我把歌声留在身后，留给那年年归来的忍冬花的繁茂，和南风的喜悦。
I leave my songs behind me to the bloom of the ever-returning honey-suckles and the joy of the wind from the south.

当枯叶在泥土里迷失自我之时,就加入了森林的生命里了。
Dead leaves when they lose themselves in soil take part in the life of the forest.

心灵一直从声音和静默里寻找它的语言,宛如天空从黑暗和光明里寻找它的语言一样。
The mind ever seeks its words from its sounds and silence as the sky from its darkness and light.

无形的黑暗吹着他的长笛,而光亮的旋律就萦绕在繁星和太阳之间,回荡在思绪和梦想里。
The unseen dark plays on his flute and the rhythm of light eddies into stars and suns, into thoughts and dreams.

我的歌儿要唱道,我已爱上"你"的歌曲了。
My songs are to sing that I have loved Thy singing.

当沉静的声音接触到我的语言时,我就认识了他,也因此认识了自己。

When the voice of the Silent touches my words, I know him and therefore I know myself.

我最后的致敬是要给那些人——他们了解我不完美却还爱着我。

My last salutations are to them who knew me imperfect and loved me.

爱的礼物是不能赠予的,它等候着被接受。

Love's gift cannot be given, it waits to be accepted.

死神来临时对我轻声说:"你的日子已经到尽头了。"
我这样对他说:"我生活在爱里而不仅在时光里。"
他会问:"你的歌还能保留下来吗?"
我会说:"我不知道,但我知道,每当我歌唱时,我就找到了我的永恒。"

When death comes and whispers to me, "Thy days are ended, "let me say to him," I have lived in love and not in mere time."
He will ask, "Will thy songs remain?"
I shall say, "I know not, but this I know that often when I sang, I found my eternity."

"让我点亮我的灯盏吧，"星星说，"永远不要争议它会不会帮助消散黑暗。"
"Let me light my lamp, "says the star," And never debate if it will help to remove the darkness."

在我的旅途结束之前，愿我能找到内心深处那个包容一切的自我，让外在的躯壳与随波逐流的众生一起随着偶然和易变的流水漂走。
Before the end of my journey may I reach within myself the one which is the all, leaving the outer shell to float away with the drifting multitude upon the current of chance and change.